Leaves

Leaves

For all-year round colour and interest in the garden

Michael Jefferson-Brown
Photographs by John Glover

DAVID & CHARLES
Newton Abbot   London

Frontispiece Cherry leaves at
the Hillier Arboretum

By the same author

The Daffodil
Daffodils for Amateurs
The Winter Garden
Modern Lilies
Daffodils, Tulips, and Hardy Bulbs
Daffodils and Narcissi
Small Garden Design
Enjoying Your Garden
The Spring Garden
Your Vines and Wines
The Lily

British Library Cataloguing in Publication Data
Jefferson-Brown, Michael, *1930*
    Leaves.
    1. Gardens. Foliage plants
    I. Title
    635.9'75

    ISBN 0-7153-9312-X

Typeset by ABM Typographics Ltd Hull
and printed in Portugal
by Resopal
for David & Charles Publishers plc
Brunel House   Newton Abbot   Devon

Contents

1   Gardening with Leaves

Senecio, 'Sunshine' is one of the most useful of silver-leaved shrubs for areas of poor soils in open sites. It will grow well by the seaside where relatively few shrubs can manage

The man who could not see the wood for the trees had a brother. This brother could not see his garden for the flowers.

At a very conservative estimate, nine-tenths of a garden is foliage. Yet it often gets scant attention. Even the most wide-eyed tend to get beguiled and blinded by the floral tenth. We need a sharper awareness of the beauty and diversity of leaves.

A flowerless world is unthinkable. Flowers give joy and inspiration. All great occasions of our lives are marked with flowers. They are a tonic for the depressed spirit. The ultimate aim of plants is to produce seed, but to us the culmination of their annual cycle is with the production of blossom. This is their showiest time. We stand, admire, and perhaps feel a glow of satisfaction that the investment of X hours of labour has come to happy fruition.

At the same time there are plants on which we descend, armed with secateurs, ready to cut away floral efforts. We are hard to please. Premiums are paid for clones of those plants that fail to bloom or which are virtually flowerless. True it is a small category. Silver-leaved wormwood is preferred with its tailored velvety fronds unspoilt by any floral frivolity. Many prefer *Senecio* 'Sunshine' without their yellow daisies although I find them a very acceptable bonus. Sempervivums with ground-hugging patterns of fleshy rosettes building up a football crowd population explosion, suddenly erupt hooliganwise to throw up quite ridiculous flowering stems.

The theme of the book is not anti-flower; no deep-seated antipathy is being exorcised. The argument is that we place so great an emphasis on the fleeting flowers that we miss the lasting delight of foliage. There must come a time when we will dash into the shop not to buy flowers but to say, 'I would like a nice bunch of foliage. What have you got?'

Gardens are becoming increasingly smaller as the price of building land continues to escalate. Talk is no longer of roods or acres, but of square feet and mortgages.

Compressed garden size concentrates great emphasis on each inhabitant. We look critically at each plant in our yards of sanctuary and accept those guaranteeing outstanding performance and unblemished respectability. Antisocial behaviour cannot be tolerated. We expect each plant to grow tidily, to bloom, and, if deciduous or herbaceous, to leave the stage with dignity and possibly with a final flourish of autumnal colour or architectural beauty in seedheads and russet foliage.

The forsythias of this world wager all on floral extravagance to gain admittance, such largesse they feel will not be denied, but they are ordinary in leaf and usually sadly undistinguished in autumn. Many annuals are passable in youth, splendid in bloom, but lax and untidy in old age. Calendulas sprawl, foliage grey with age. Each

The New Zealand flax *Phormium tenax* 'Variegatum', with a yellow geum, and fleshy-leaved *Sedum spectabile (Author)*

plant is in leaf by far the greatest proportion of the year. However splendid the bloom, we ought first to direct our attention to the foliage. Horticultural writers dwell on harmonies or contrasts of flower colours. This is not unimportant but, having ascertained that our plants are suited to soil and site, the first consideration is to arrange our foliage.

A simple little arrangement in a small plot in front of a house could be created with three basic conifers in distinct forms and colours. A spire-shaped conifer like the Irish juniper, *Juniperus communis* 'Hibernica' or 'Skyrocket' would give the main vertical feel contrasting to the horizontal spreading form of another juniper like 'Silver Spreader' or *J. horizontalis* 'Blue Chip'. Then our old friend *Thuja occidentalis* 'Rheingold' could provide a comfortable broad conical shape of gold sometimes bronzed. Around these one could plant different-coloured heathers and simple things like *Sedum maximum*.

The gardener is god to the plot. The masterplan is to maximise the contribution of each plant and create a unified whole. Plant associations become important; the strong sword-like leaves of iris contrast with rough furry dark clustered leaves of geums and the succulent spoon-shaped efforts of *Sedum maximum*. But it is not only the mix of things vegetative that can accentuate each other's character. Contrasts of the inanimate with the growing plant can be extraordinarily effective. Large-leaved ivy might clamber through some balustrading, the stone highlighting the patterns of leaf and stem, whilst ivy enhances the atmosphere of age and permanence.

Design and Planning

Garden plans may be simple in the extreme. There may seem to be a total lack of plan. Cottage gardens are collections of happy accidents. Vegetable garden foliage can give joy before it reaches the table. Onions, like soldiers on parade, contrast with the splendid rounded completeness of cabbage and the gothic splendour of curly kale.

Most dominant feature of most sites is going to be the living house. We can marry house to garden by planting shrubs close by and making use of the wall shelter to grow *Iris unguicularis, Gladiolus nanus,* and others that crave extra warmth. Walls are clothed with climbing plants. Roses reach to bedroom windows. Juliet plucks a blossom or two whilst Romeo labours with fork in the herbaceous border. On one of the walls a mature specimen of *Actinidia kolomikta* produces its exciting multicoloured foliage purplish in youth and then green, white and pink. Here a corner gives support to the three-lobed polished dark-green leaves of the early flowering *Clematis armandii,* one of the very few evergreen climbing shrubs.

Mistaken choice of wallpaper on the inside walls can be annoying but relatively quickly remedied. Outside we cannot afford too many mistakes. Shrubs covering the wall may be there for life, that is, your life! Shall we plant a Virginia creeper? It loses its leaves early in the autumn and, although so early to bed, it is in no hurry to be early to rise. However it provides such a vivid autumn spectacle it has to be given space somewhere. No flower border can equal its flashing flaming golds, oranges, and crimsons before we cart away the discarded brilliance. It has the good manners to strip quickly unlike wisterias and others that take weeks to disrobe.

The house must be thought about. We look from it and at it. More visually dominant may be neighbouring buildings, walls, and fences that divide and surround our domain. Next in importance may be the paths.

We plan Eden to have no vistas dominated by surrounding buildings. These shall be masked by evergreen and deciduous jungle. Less-pleasing fences shall be lost behind shrubs grouped to provide mixed colour, to give the effect of light and shade even on the dullest of days. Variegated hollies, weigelas, and aucubas jostle with dark-leaved rhododendrons and camellias, whilst sparkling eucalyptus flash silver and metallic grey from flat-leaved everclothed branches.

Hard lines of pathways are softened by cushions of artemisias, the leathery rounded leaves of bergenias almost large enough to play table tennis with, and the leaning silver grey of lavender. The garden shed has been lost beneath a knitted tangle of Russian vine. Perhaps it would have been wiser to use something choicer — roses, honeysuckles, and clematis, but certainly nothing would have grown so quickly. Garbage bin screens are themselves clothed by cotoneasters.

Buildings to be screened may demand the planting of a group of trees. Small gardens cannot have large trees; some, like Lombardy poplars, are shallow rooted and can be dangerous too close to houses. Screening can be evergreen masses. Conifers come to the forefront of our thinking. It may be wise to pause before stationing a company of these at the boundary to block out the gasworks.

Eye and brain have an unusual relationship. Eyes signal a part of something seen, the brain makes good the rest and makes sense of the whole. Familiarity with a sight or sound can dull appreciation. We move into a fresh room and note a mark on the wall to be over-printed. Having failed to take immediate action, in a few days we fail to notice the mark.

Similarly the stark outlines of a building can often be more quickly and effectively screened by planting rapidly growing deciduous trees than conifers. The lines of the tree branches arch over the silhouette of the building. The relentless straight lines of the structure are broken and the eye no longer scans up, down and across but explores the more interesting, closer pattern of the tree. It may well be that conifers planted to the side of an offending sight will provide an alternative focal point that will gain greater ascendancy as the trees grow.

Planting towards the extremes of your boundary may be sensible if not conflicting with your neighbour's rights. The closer an object

LEFT
Fig *(Ficus carica)* with its
handsome large-fingered
leaves, here with the spurge
Euphorbia characias
'Wulfenii', and wisteria on the
far wall *(Denmans)*

ABOVE
This bold planting of
Juniperus sabina
'Tamariscifolia' in the
foreground helps to set off
the dramatic tree, *Acer
negundo* 'Variegatum'

is to the observer the larger it is as a proportion of the view. A modest tree planted near the most frequent vantage point may provide more screening than a fair-sized forest in the middle distance.

A foliar screen could be of mixed conifers and deciduous trees grouped together. Two important advantages accrue to the mixed approach. Changing seasons and passing years will bring far greater variety, interest and beauty. This is the bolder idea. Dark foliage backs a lemony-leaved tree, formal conical growth gives added point to the spreading cloud-shaped mass of another. The weeping tree is made more telling by the strong ascending arms of its neighbours.

Aesthetic points proliferate and form the major portion of our thinking, but practical points also bolster the argument for mixed plantings. A uniform line of trees is impressive, each leaf unfurled to order. The fifth tree becomes diseased and has to be felled. The missing tooth gapes. But it could be worse still, trouble spreading, a Dutch Elm type disease taking the lot. Safer by far to spread the chances. Lesser troubles, such as severe winter weather searing the sides of conifers, confines the affliction to the few and does not involve wholesale disfiguration.

Choosing Trees and Shrubs

Having arranged any necessary screening we can now start to plant trees, pass on to shrubs, and end with things of lesser stature.

Eucalyptus niphophila (centre), silver blue-grey *Thalictrum flavum glaucum* (back), *Aucuba japonica* (spotted laurel) (left), *Brunnera macrophylla* (front), dwarf conifer *Thuja* 'Rheingold', and *Rhododendrum*

The larger the tree the more impact it can make and the more important it is to get it in the right spot. Within reason we choose the largest but this is not a plea for a forest tree — its place is in a forest. Plantings need to be to scale. Cherries and apples are often the right size. Other larger trees are relatively slow growing so they will not be a problem in one's lifetime. Some trees can be thought of as renewable in the sense that they may be brought low and allowed to regrow as pollarded specimens. On a fairly modest scale a hazel, perhaps the dark maroon purple-leaved *Corylus maxima* 'Purpurea' can be reduced to stumps a few inches high. It will take this treatment as a challenge and shoot up thickets of upright branches but with lesser arching ones. All will be clothed with massively enlarged maxi-leaves of dramatically deep colour. Even catkins are purple. The ordinary hazel, *C. avellana* and its variety 'Purpurea', are vigorous enough but *C. maxima* is far stronger.

Other energetic growers may not regard the saw or secateur as the end of life. The eucalpts, *E. gunnii, E. niphophila* and some others, are not always that easy to kill. The sight of soot-black bare main trunks of eucalyptus trees after a bush fire was depressing until we realised that a miracle of resurrection was taking place with bunches of fresh growth bursting at intervals up the charred poles. A eucalyptus stump will normally throw a goodly number of upright branches decked in the attractive juvenile foliage, round as silver coins in the case of *E. gunnii*. This species can be pollarded every few seasons. Alternatively all competing branches can be allowed their head and a fascinating multi-trunked specimen formed, similar but more exotic than similar many-trunked silver birches.

Eucalyptus species will grow well in dry poor soils. *E. niphophila* could be planted with some smaller companions. *Euphorbia characias* 'Wulfenii' is evergreen and makes an interesting grey-green harmony with the eucalyptus. The low mass of a *Viburnum davidii* will be a dark-green contrast, whilst the tiny leaves of heathers make a change of texture. A clump of hostas will give a broad leaf change in shape. Although primarily thought of as plants for moist areas, many will do reasonably well in quite dry spots.

Specimen trees need picking with care. They should be attractive at all times. Almonds that are fluorescent pink in early spring soon lose their blossom and with it all claim to distinction. Silver birches are light and pleasing with moving and flickering foliage. Cut-leaved *Betula pendula* 'Crispa' has an even lighter touch. Its branches weep but the main trunk grows upright. Like some others it will shed leaves and small twigs at almost all times of year creating small but irritating job opportunities. The contorted willow, *Salix matsudana* 'Tortuosa' is another that one can admire but also curse repeatedly for its litterlout habit. Best plant it away from carefully tended areas. Altogether better in this respect is *Robinia pseudoacacia* 'Frisia'. It soon makes a reasonably sized tree of graceful habit with fine light-golden foliage that looks fresh and pleasing at all times.

Weeping willows are only permissible where there is plenty of

LEFT
The popular suburban tree
Robinia pseudoacacia 'Frisia'
contrasted with the dark and
vigorous herbaceous
Macleaya cordata (left). The
bright small-leaved *Lonicera
nitida* 'Baggesen's Gold'
completes the trio *(Greatham
Mill)*

ABOVE
Hostas are leading foliage
plants now highly fashionable.
Here are the light *H.fortunei
aurea* with the blue-green
*H.sieboldiana. Meconopsis
grandis* is flowering at the
back

room. A planting scheme with some of the same atmospheric effect could be achieved with the smaller somewhat weeping willowed-leaved pear, *Pyrus salicifolia,* which one could underplant with red-stemmed dogwood *Cornus alba, Geranium psilostemon, Alchemilla mollis,* and heathers. For evergreen shrubby colour and mass, a golden conifer will make a useful bright effect to back the red winter stems of the dogwood and to lighten the effect of *Viburnum tinus* with its rounded form of dark green enlivened with pink and white posies of flowers through the winter months.

Evergreen masses of junipers, either as upright columns or widely flaring, approach architectural solidarity and tidiness. They come in made-to-measure sizes and styles. Other conifers are as tidy and as sculptural. One may even decide to try something quite different as a focal point. Statuesque clumps of bamboo are opulent and atmospheric and do not drop leaves.

Whilst looking at the broad canvas we see trees as a foliar mass, but certain species soon stand out, recognised for their beauty as a whole but also where the contribution of their leaves is paramount. Our eye delights in size, texture, shape, and colour. Plane trees in cities hold a balance between the attraction of the whole and delight in the leaf. The pocket-handkerchief tree, *Davidia involucrata,* makes a good orthodox tree-shaped tree. Leaf size attracts, even in the absence of the huge, waving white bracts that make the mature specimen such a feature. In this same vein the Golden Indian bean tree, *Catalpa bignonioides* 'Aurea', is a wide-angled, relatively sparingly branched tree hung with large, simple ovate leaves. Shining lemon gold in youth, a touch more green in maturity, they become a mellow gold before falling. Such a colour against the black green of a yew is delightful.

Almost miniature palm-like evergreen *Mahonia* 'Charity'

The airspace above is important in any garden design. We hook the sky into the picture by growing trees upwards.

Shrubs bring fresh opportunities and some limitations. We walk around, we see them from above or at eye level. There is less chance of cutting designs out of the sky. Propinquity allows us to play with colours, to contrast textures, or accentuate the framework of horizontal-stretching *Viburnum plicatum* 'Lanarth', the arching *Cotoneaster franchetii,* the cascading *Pyrus salicifolia,* and the upright-armed branches of *Berberis hakeoides.* Rusty gold of *Thuja occidentalis* 'Rheingold' is built into a pyramid whilst *Salix repens* 'Argentea' has silver foliage on arching stems that scramble over the ground. Here *Mahonia* 'Charity' has stems upright as guardsmen. Flowers are a conspicuous concession, not blanco coloured, but lemon-scented pale-yellow sprays in early and into deep midwinter. Some shrubs are mundane; no one gets excited about forsythia foliage or the leaves of lilacs, but other shrubs are attractive from youth to the multicoloured swansong of old age. Japanese maples belong to this company.

Shrubs may well form the backbone of garden design. They grow, they change, they fulfil their potential, they give shape and continuity to the garden scene.

Herbaceous Plants

Now come the herbaceous plants. They start from nought each season, encompassing the unfurling of young foliage (a slow sequence with such things as ferns and paeonies), the transformation of the often bright-coloured young tissue to its fully mature state to support the expanding plant and its effort to reproduce via the flowering performance. Old age may be dignified or an ignominious collapse and the husbanding of resources below ground for another year. The show never stops. Hostas like *H. fortunei* 'Aurea' can spear through the soil, then unfurl their pattern of broad leaves all bright light gold edged in green. In maturity the yellow becomes greener but before the leaves die they celebrate old age in gold. Flowers are modestly pretty but of secondary interest just as the metallic foliage of some thalictrums, all patterns of delight, outclasses the plumes of itsy-bitsy flowers that overtop all physically but rather let the side down.

A bed could be composed of three columns of *Prunus* 'Amanogawa' or 'Spire' to give height and vertical strength. Various low-growing plants like prostrate junipers can provide evergreen ground cover together with herbaceous carpeters, such as the bugles (ajugas). Dark-leaved smoke bush, *Cotinus coggygria* 'Royal Purple' or a similar variety, will be dramatic in the growing months and can be highlighted by something as simple as golden privet which will be useful as a cut-and-come-again item for augmenting indoor displays. *Ligularia przewalskii* has large dark leaves and stems which can be a major contrast to the dwarfer ornamental grasses or epimediums.

These good companions are arrow-head leaved *Epimedium grandiflorum*, blue-green sweeping branches of *Juniperus horizontalis*, dark round-leaved *Cotinus* 'Royal Purple', narrowly fastigiate *Prunus* 'Spire', golden privet *Ligustrum ovalifolium* 'Aureum', *Yucca filamentosa*, bold-leaved dark-stemmed *Ligularia przewalskii*, and carpeting *Ajuga reptans*

Ardent advocacy of ground-covering plants sometimes gives us pause to think. We are wary of the overcommitted. There is a case, though, for ground cover which is looked at in a later chapter. Visually soil-hugging plants can complement their upwardly mobile neighbours. Spikes of foxtail lilies (eremurus) glisten and gleam in the sunshine, a contrast to the hostas, senecios and elaeagnus below.

The lowly play their role. They shade the bulbs of the lily. It is a co-operative effort. Patterns of variegated *Weigela* could not be more distinct from the smart whorled foliage of *Lilium pardalinum*.

We begin to see more clearly the leaf and the leaves, and appreciate their changing character as they pass through the annual cycle. Neighbouring plants, structure, contour, lighting, all play their part. Here sunlight strikes through the canopy and highlights golden foliage. By the waterside the form of leaf and colour is reflected. Here is magic. Breezes blow and the black poplar flashes silver-mirror-backed leaves. The birches ripple.

The whole is alive, moving, changing and growing. Colours in the evening light are more subtle and perhaps more beautiful. 'Look your last on all things lovely, every hour,' wrote Walter de la Mare. We shall look. It has been a world of wonder. When we rise in the morning, there will have been change; it is a fresh universe.

OPPOSITE
The unusual squirrel-tail grass *Hordeum jubatum*, in summer, with its silken shimmering spikes.

Cotinus coggygria 'Foliis Purpureis', one of the smoke trees. The cultivar 'Royal Purple' is similar, even richer in colour, and the most widely available. Maroon-purple foliage is contrasted with a golden conifer and the grey-leaved *Eucalyptus gunnii* (Author)

2   *A Look at the Material*

First there is colour; shape, texture, and pose come later. Greens we expect to see and, because of that expectation, we hardly notice their infinite variety. Of all colours this is the most important; we could garden with this colour alone, but it is not alone, a full palette awaits the painting of our leafy picture. Many orthodox green leaves have coloured mutants. Green conifers have golden and bronzed relatives. Large-leaved *Catalpa bignonioides*, the Indian bean, has its golden counterpart, 'Aurea', resplendent against dark spires of conifers.

Lots of silver leaves are green overlaid with a coat of fine silky hairs to look white or silver. Some leaves have their surfaces so densely powdered with meal as to be albino. 'Dusty Miller' auriculas are one instance. Farinosa group primulas are characterised by this white meal. Tiny *P. farinosa* and its even tinier relative, *P. scotica*, are rare natives of some British hills, but, being so small, can scarcely become foliage plants, except in the miniature arrangements of trough gardens, or rock beds where closer observation is the rule.

A popular foliar variation is a change to reddish purple. There may be argument about the advisability of planting copper beeches. Colour depths vary, some clones can be very dark indeed. Beeches are amongst the most splendid of trees, but whether the dark-coloured forms are needed in wholesale quantities may be questioned. One may cause excitement in a wide landscape; groups in the countryside are too exotic for our gentle landscape. It is a forest tree that does not belong in a small garden. If there is an irresistible urge to plant a beech, a fastigiate one will be more manageable.

More domestic in scale is the widely used *Prunus* 'Pissardii' with its bonus of early pale-pink blossom. It looks well in a mixed planting, but some find it a dull tree, lacking the polished leaf surface of the beech. Some of the dark-leaved apples are a different matter; the dark mature leaves are often lit up by brighter tones of new unfurling youngsters, bright coral or salmon.

Cotinus coggygria 'Royal Purple' and other named forms, are very effective. They contribute as new purchased fledglings and steadily become more inspiring as they grow to maturity. Leaves are rounded and flat, neatly displayed on longish stalks, and, depending on the clone, varying in colour, some having a reddish cast. They maintain a freshness from youth till the autumn striptease. It is the texture and clear-cut form of the foliage that helps this species so much, a contrast to *Prunus* 'Pissardii' with its dark crinkled leaves. Whilst still worth growing as a tree amongst others, the prunus lacks the freshness of the *Cotinus*.

We are reliably informed that the Assyrians came down with their cohorts 'gleaming in purple and gold.' Purple foliage could look oppressive deployed to excess, but is effective as spot plants of con-

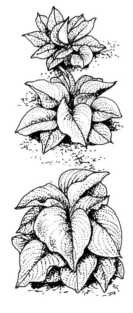

Sculptured forms of *Hosta sieboldii* can make one of the most abstract of patterns in the garden, in tones of grey, silver, blue and green

trasting colour and tone. The darkness of copper beech, purple-black malus, cotinus, and others, need the company of brighter, lighter fellows. Following the Assyrians we dress our cohorts in gold as well as purple. Here is dramatic contrast, complementary on the colour spectrum, the golds being much paler toned so that each highlights the other. No need to plant the rare and expensive; here *Berberis thunbergii* 'Atropurpurea' contrasts with the golden privet. Similar drama is enacted by the dark cut-leaved maple, *Acer palmatum* 'Atropurpureum', and the golden-leaved hosta, *H. fortunei* 'Aurea'.

Few plants are completely yellow in leaf, although there is an extensive parade of golden conifers. Leaving the conifers aside for the moment, pause to praise a commoner whose virtues are often taken for granted. For many years we have never been without golden privet in the borders. Bright and cheerful the year round, it is a most useful plant for cutting to augment flower arrangements. Pruning encourages plenty of fresh young growth with clean gilded leaves. We have a bush reaching to flash golden brilliance below silver *Eucalyptus gunnii* and next to purple-stemmed ligularias with broad leaves biting into space with wicked teeth. As easy to grow and as evergold, is the bright tiny-leaved *Lonicera nitida* 'Baggesen's Gold'.

Case for Variegation
Nature usually spends gold sparingly, gilding the edges of leaves or

Easy dogwood *Cornus alba* 'Elegantissima', its greens and creams making it one of the most effective of light variegated shrubs

ABOVE
Japanese maples in the
Japanese Garden at Compton
Acres, Poole, Dorset. The
foliage of these acers is
pleasing at all stages, and as
specimens mature they form
elegant shapes

RIGHT
Aralia elata 'Variegata' is
magnificent with pinnate
leaves often well over 1m
(3ft) long and bright with
creamy variegation. Seen
here in flower, with a
variegated ivy and glossy
bergenia *(RHS Wisley)*

arranging variegation. There are several excellent hollies in gold and green, very good year-round garden value not just to be plundered at Christmas.

Deciduous *Aralia elata* varieties with huge pinnate leaves are some of the most magnificent of foliage plants. Both gold and silver variegated forms are lovely; probably my favourite variegated plants. Small plants are expensive but a sound investment. You have something extra special to give joy for many years growing steadily larger and more imposing. Some full-sized trees, like *Acer negundo* 'Elegantissimum' grow quickly and, if you are happy with such wholesale masses of variegation, this robust tree will provide a lit-up spectacle, useful counterbalance to the dark columns of conifers.

The vogue for grey- and silver-leaved plants continues. These are eye-catching, especially from late spring through to the autumn; in winter they may be sorry masses. They range from the silver-grey New Zealand carpeters, the minutely leaved ground-hugging raoulias, to aspiring giants like the eucalypts. At Burford House, Tenbury Wells, *Eucalyptus gunnii* is planted against the mass of *Cotinus* 'Royal Purple'. The contrast is dramatic. Silver-leaved plants come in the chapter on herbaceous plants as well as in the review of trees and shrubs.

Mutation or disease can cause plants to produce patterned foliage. Often leaf margins are left free of chorophyll and so display white, shades of cream, or yellow. Some gardeners feel such effects artificial and refuse to allow the variegated any roothold at all. I understand this attitude; various virus diseases can cause discoloured foliage and to a life-long nurseryman virus is a constant threat. Little wonder some plant lovers find variegated leaves, if not aesthetically offensive, a cause for unease. I was anti-variegation in the past, but now take the view that many are useful for extra colour and excitement.

There is a wide spectrum amongst the variegated cast. To be variegated is not necessarily to be of the elite. Some, like aralias already briefly lauded, are megastars, but others are very pedestrian. Some hostas and some elaeagnus species come precious close to this. Newly discovered variegated plants tempt nurserymen who see this new clone as a pot of pure gold.

A few plants are naturally bicoloured in leaf, no mutation or disease is involved. Some arums have huge arrow-head leaves, all glossy green but marked with purple. *Pulmonaria* has forms with hairy leaves, darkly spotted mauve or purple. *Tulipa greigii* has leaves most extraordinarily striped rich maroon purple. The hybrid 'Red Riding Hood' is gorgeous enough in brilliant bloom but the stylish leaf blades, in metallic grey-green, heavily overpainted in broad longitudinal purple stripes, make it one of the top selling tulips each autumn.

Enter the Surgeon

Hazels respond well to the knife. By reducing the plants to a stool only a few inches high every second or third season, the proportion

Particularly effective in the spring are the green and yellow swords of *Iris pseudacoris* 'Variegata'. As the summer advances the yellow gives way to green

of smaller inner twigs carrying less well-coloured foliage is reduced as well as ensuring individual leaves of the largest possible size.

Another shrub that behaves best under a similar regime is the golden elder. Once established, this is often best razed to the ground each winter, to encourage its ample vigour into an annual massive leap with upright arching growth and leaves of doubled, trebled, or quadrupled size in rich glowing yellow. This is a good natured simple garden shrub able to make a really worthwhile contribution to the scene without the weedy, seeding propensity of the wild elderberry. Pruning such shrubs can be done in a swash-buckling mood that can be as good as a game of squash for getting rid of pent-up feelings.

A list of shrubs and trees that can be coppiced or pollarded to give extra fine and magnified foliage includes the following:

Ailanthus altissima	*Rhus g. laciniata*
Corylus avellana 'Purpurea'	*R. typhina*
C. maxima 'Purpurea'	*R. t. laciniata*
Eucalyptus in variety	*Rubus thibetanus*
Paulownia tomentosa	*Sambucus nigra* 'Aurea'
Rhus glabra	*S. n.* 'Guincho Purple'

Colours apart, the main features noticed about most leaves are their size and shape. Size may vary from the pinhead dimensions of some things like raoulias to the huge productions of gunneras that

Paulownia tomentosa whose leaves may be naturally as much as 15-30cm (6-12in) wide and long, but by pruning (see text) they may be encouraged to a fantastic 0.60-1m (2-3ft). Below is *Nicotinia langsdorfii,* attractive in leaf and flower *(Author)*

are several feet across, often large enough to shelter underneath whilst a sudden rainstorm passes overhead. Shape is almost infinitely variable. The main forms have been given names. These are listed here with diagrams. Few gardeners will want to learn the lot, but it is useful to have a point of reference to make sense of the more botanically written plant descriptions that one comes across.

The margins of the leaves are described as entire if they are not broken by any saw edge protrusions; the ones that are jagged are described as serrated.

Leaf Forms

Plant form and colouring are the dominant factors governing the gardener's thinking in setting the stage. Consideration of size and shape of leaves will follow closely, and then thought will be given to the pose of the foliage. Sometimes branch form dictates leaf arrangement as with the horizontal branches of *Viburnum tomentosum* 'Mariesii' and the variety 'Lanarth', but sometimes leaves themselves

Magnificent rosettes of *Verbascum broussa* leaves, before these biennial plants send up their tall stems of tightly clasped yellow flowers *(Denmans)*

effect this matter of pose. Eucalypts are especially good at this, whether it be in the rounded juvenile foliage of many like that of *E. gunnii,* or their single plane flat adult leaves, often metallic in appearance and forming an intricate mobile.

Tough dark leaves of camellias, polished to a high-gloss finish, mark one end of the range of leaf textures. Texture is something we usually sense, but to which we pay too little direct attention. We should allow our senses greater rein in such matters; to touch rosemary or lavender when passing is not unbridled hedonism and to stroke the juniper is as sensible as petting the cat.

Rhododendrons are so many and so different that generalisation could be ridiculous. Unending masses of *R. ponticum* can be depressing, but many species and hybrids have splendid polished upper surfaces and lower ones covered with a thick felt, often in a rich, chocolate, rusty shade. Varying sizes, colours, and poses should ensure that a rhododendron collection is interesting when there is no hint of a flower.

The opposite extreme in leaf textures is represented by the woolly or furry-leaved brethren, such as the lamb's tongue, *Stachys byzantina.* Such silvery leaves are usually given their glittering sheen by the light playing on fine hairs. Some hairy types can look woebegone during the dull days of winter, but all is redeemed in spring with fresh growth.

Thick, leathery leaves of bergenias and tough, succulent arms of agaves contrast with the floating light foliage of such plants as fen-

Leaf shapes:
 1 Linear
 2 Lanceolate
 3 Oblanceolate
 4 Ovate
 5 Obovate
 6 Elliptical
 7 Spatulate
 8 Sagittate
 9 Hastate
10 Cordate
11 Reniform
12 Pinnate
13 Palmate

Margins:
14 Entire
15 Serate
16 Dentate
17 Cemulate
18 Lobed
19 Parted
20 Dissected

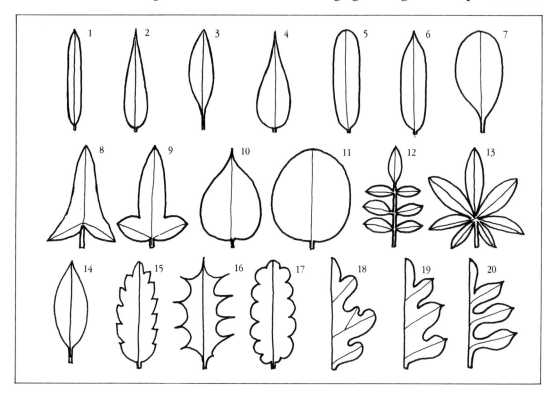

nel, asparagus, many ferns, or even trees like the robinias. Not so succulent, but just as tough looking, are the clumps of *Yucca filamentosa,* completely hardy and with dark sword leaves on guard all round. A useful architectural plant, evergreen, formidable, it is usually completely reliable in the matter of producing tall creamy flower spikes. Do not believe that it only blooms every five or seven years. Young plants will produce lots of flower spikes.

Sometimes a leaf surface is like embossed leather; the popular *Viburnum fragrans* and the hybrids with *V. grandiflorum,* the *V. x bodnantense* kinds 'Dawn' and 'Deben', have their network of veins somewhat sunken. It is more noticeable in the evergreen *V. rhytidophyllum,* a shrub that can look impressive in a rather staid, Victorian manner. Dark, long leaves are clearly embossed with the pattern of veins. Our own specimens of this species eventually were dug up. I believe there are various clones of this and the leaves on the plants we had fostered drooped with the same grace as socks hanging out to dry. I have seen many that looked far more perky and attractive.

A pleasing embossed-leaved plant is a small prostrate willow, *Salix reticulata*, its name acknowledging the feature of the foliage. Forget the stereotype willow leaf, this is different. Plants grow on the rocky tops of some Scottish hills and in the Alps. Branches hug the ground and the leaves that burst the fat buds, silvery in their first days, form tough, glossy, rich-green leaves as rounded as table-tennis bats, and patterned with a network of veins. In a dampish place in the rock garden, bed, or trough garden, it looks very distinctive. It has relatives with attractive foliage. Wide silver-grey leaves of *S. lanata* have their veins clearly defined so adding to their general attractiveness. But of willows more anon.

Happy accidents may promote effective associations, but start by trying some obvious ploys to accentuate the characters of plants in juxtaposition. Thus the furry silver carpet of *Stachys byzantina* fronts the broad flat upright fans of a strong iris or the darker swords of yuccas.

Branching habits of shrubs and trees dictate much of the disposition of their leaves. The flat herringbone fashion of *Cotoneaster horizontalis* is a dimension away from the fastigiate uprightness of *Prunus* 'Spire'. *Viburnum davidii,* making steady horizontal growth, with relatively large evergreen leaves, amasses a form of eminent respectability. To the rear a weeping willow has almost a curtain of golden hanging wands, the long leaves hanging and maintaining the overall design. Here a clump of bamboo reaches strongly upwards, balanced by leaves at varying angles. Bamboos can add a rather unusual element in the garden plan, their angularity being an arresting difference to the usual pattern of curving lines.

The solidity of the conifer columns and spires can be given even greater architectural weight by the contrasting lightness of trees such as birches and poplars, whose leaves and branches wave in even the lightest of breezes. Too many dark conifers suggest a mausoleum; a balance needs to be maintained. Movement introduced into the garden will help to banish all risk of lifelessness. Some willows, such as the weeping ones, the twisty *Salix matsudana* 'Tortuosa', or the purple-stemmed *S. daphnoides* are rarely still.

Water is another element that provides the atmosphere of the garden. A still sheet of water reflects the foliar masses, but water is rarely mirror-still. Rippling effects give movement and intriguing patterns. Running water, by sound and sight, almost shouts of liveliness. Waterside situations can often have accentuated light and shade effects. Light playing on the water can highlight leaf pose and form. Bullrushes and irises spear heavenwards; ferns arch over with intricate tracery and larger leaves such as gunneras come into their own. Rodgersias romp, some with bronzed large leaves reminiscent of horse chestnuts. In the water a community of plants lives in a creative balance. Water-lily pads float in rounded patterns alive in air and water. Acres of water draw people with a magnetic force, but a small area can also exert a powerful influence. The magic of fire and water captivates young children, and not all of us grow out of such simple fascination. A garden with water and a bonfire site is just a few yards this side of heaven.

Monumental *Yucca filamentosa* 'Variegata' with *Hosta fortunei aurea* (foreground), and the conifer *Chamaecyparis obtusa*

3 *The Changing Seasons*

Gardening is an art form. Not all gardeners are great artists, but fortunately the living materials we work with often blot out design mistakes. The accidental is often as telling as the carefully manipulated idea.

A painting or sculpture is complete when the last touch is added, it becomes static and unchanging and only the attitudes of viewers may change. A musical composition comes to life when played, like a book the score may be taken up and rerun but afterwards it lies dormant. There is very little dormant in a garden.

Our acres or hectares, few square metres or square yards, viewed as works of art, fall in a different category. They are ever-present and ever-changing. Plants grow, die and are replaced as the years pass; the small tree that the children jumped over becomes a near giant. Every day the aspect differs; wind, rain, sunshine, frost and snow play a part but in temperate areas the seasons exercise the major influence by changing the character and importance of each plant. The herbaceous go through rapid changes, but conifers, whilst being evergreen, have their seasons too. New growth casts a sheen over all, even where the new closely matches the colour of the old growth. Some colour variants become more golden during the

New Zealand flax *Phormium*, the deciduous *Viburnum plicatum tomentosum* (back), flower arrangers' standby *Alchemilla mollis* (front), and the unfurling fronds of hart's tongue fern, *Asplenium scolopendrium*

growing months. In winter many take on quite a different cast, some green kinds assuming a mauve or purple look whilst others like *Thuja occidentalis* 'Rheingold' can have their gold alloyed by bronze and rust.

The gardener has a more wonderful palette than any painter. Each leaf will respond to its environment; the soil, the accompanying plants, the play of light from above, are all influenced by the gardener. The masterplan is to make the most of each passing season and foliage is the major changing component in the changing design.

Super Spring

At no time are eyes so sharp and eager to see evidence of change and growth as in the spring. We wait for the curtain to go up on a new season, a new growing year. The spring of the countryside is splendid; in the garden we aim not only to accentuate every pleasing aspect but to persuade the earliest possible manifestation of the season. Plants have been brought back from all over the world to try to elbow winter out of the way. Breeders, too, have striven to develop earlier daffodils and tulips, to have livelier primroses and polyanthus and select shrub and tree forms that dare to start into attractive activity as soon as winter relaxes its hold. Spring will be glorious in the countryside; in the garden it will be Super Spring.

The new growth may be floral, but mostly leaf and stem burst into activity. The freshness of colour and texture in their quantity and quality are unique to spring. The range is wide. Sometimes the eye misses a feature because familiarity has bred blindness or because some exciting growth is hidden away. We need to plan to show off plants by placing them in contrasting or harmonising juxtaposition. Colour, form, mass, and texture all play their part.

All maples have good leaves. *Acer palmatum's* many forms range from boldly lobed kinds to some so heavily indented as to become filigree designs with veins only narrowly accompanied by leaf tissue

Simple things can be very effective. Daffodil foliage is unexciting in old age, but a clump just thrusting upwards through the soil is full of urgent promise, quite different in character from the nearby bush of *Rosa rubrifolia* with its slender armed branches marking an intricate pattern that will be lost behind the neat reddish mauve foliage that will unfurl from swelling buds. This in its turn will mask the untidiness of the ageing daffodil foliage. Later, hostas are impressive as new growth cuts its way with sharp pointed buds becoming cylinders before the leaf unfurls.

The new foliage colours of some trees and shrubs are remarkable. We look afresh at greens such as that of the newly unwrapped larch. It seems to be the living quintessence of greenness. Below, the evergreen *Pieris formosa* 'Forrestii' is putting on new growth but one can be forgiven if, from a distance it is mistaken for blossom, the young pointed leaves and stems are a vivid crimson scarlet made even more showy and resplendent against the dark green, older foliage by its sparkling high-gloss finish. Few flowers could do as well. Other evergreens have their moments of glory. Late in the spring and through the summer the young foliage of eucalypts is most beautiful. *E. gunnii* is the top favourite with gardener and

Striking young foliage of the dwarf shrub *Aesculus neglecta* 'Erythroblastos', a relative of the horse chestnut, though often content with a height of 2m (6ft)

flower arranger with its rounded juvenile leaves glistening mauvy pink as well as bright silver; rose-madder painted stems complement the colours. Leaves of the hardiest of all eucalypts, *E. niphophila,* come red, orange, and maroon with pinky-orange leaf stalks and stems becoming white with bloom. The golden privet's newly minted leaves are of bright gold while the catkins and young leaves of the sturdy-stemmed dwarfish willow, *Salix lanata*, are encased in finest spun silver and gold.

It is the combination of colour and texture that wins. We delight in watching the unfolding of the sticky buds of horse chestnut brought from outside to develop earlier under our admiring scrutiny inside. The sticky bracts, the silken-haired stems and the fresh young leaves make a marvellous picture. Some of the larger acers are just as wonderful and should be tried also.

The maples as tree or shrub are famous for their foliar beauty. Spring is all vivid freshness, summer is splendour, and autumn is a fantastic party time. The Japanese have long cultivated maples and have raised multitudes of new ones. A garden could be created out of a collection of *A. palmatum* forms alone, an unending variety of leaf form and colour. They may be slow to start growing, no ex-

The brilliant young foliage of evergreen *Pieris* 'Forest Flame'

trovert forsythias these, but they make steady progress and are pleasing in all sizes, even the tiny newly purchased one. Forget the price you paid, it was expensive but it will prove worthwhile. These maples do best in the least bleak spots, as severe frosts and cutting winds can damage young leaves that have yet to gain their full hardiness.

Some herbaceous and alpine plants grow out of silken swaddling as do some ferns. *Pulsatilla vulgaris (Anemone pulsatilla)* erupts into growth, all unfurling leaves, stems and flowerbuds clothed with silken down. *P.vernalis* as it expands from winter's rest is furry as a kitten. Species of the great buttercup family, *Ranunculaceae,* are clean shaven to the extent of appearing polished and lacquered. The paeonies that rocket out of the ground can have stems of rich crimson almost as pleasing in their season as the flowers in their brief passage.

The glistening freshness of much new foliage is redolent of the promised future. It may be on a small or large scale. The shining embossed rounded leaves of *Salix reticulata* have this pristine newborn quality. The same newborn feeling is present with the unfurling large glossy leaves of *Rodgersia aesculifolia* sparkling so that each facet of the reticulate leaf catches the light at a different angle. Here the freshness is allied to a rich, bronze-red suffused colour.

Later spring sees all the trees and shrubs in action; some, like most vines, delay their start, but once aroused sprint into growth to make up for lost time. The purple-leaved *Vitis vinifera* 'Purpurea' and varieties of the domestic grape such as 'Brandt', grown as much for their foliage and autumn colours as for their unexciting fruit, will race over any support around. While pruning vines we have measured annual growths well over twenty feet long. The young stems and leaves shine full of the pressing sap that fuels their energy. The huge-leaved *V.coignetiae* has the same athletic character. We look to see whether we shall have leaves as large or larger than the foot long ones we measured last year. If a little pruning has been done, it is likely that the channelled vigour will threaten records. The true Virginia creeper, *Parthenocissus quinquefolia*, and its relatives *P.henryana* and the very popular *P.tricuspidata* are also late starters but, once into growth, the walls that were bare one day are soon covered with glistening fresh minted leaves. Growth can be seen clearly day by day. The same plant that covers a north wall and reaches round an angle to the west- or south-facing sides presents the unusual sight of bursting buds and young leaves on the warmer walls whilst those on the north wall are still tight.

Plants pruned in autumn and winter, make dramatic growth, coming as if from a sprinter's starting block. The hybrid roses, so many thorny sticks one minute, soon produce succulent stems and clean new leaves. The usual hybrid kinds can be brilliantly green, red or purple. To my mind, a few weeks into the new season is the finest hour of many of these plants. All is clean and full of promise, no black spot or mildew or blown flowers. They are unattractive during winter and this tells against them in my book. The ramblers, shrub roses, and species or species hybrids can be a very different matter. These can have architectural value and the foliage be pleasing. The early small-scale light-green leaves of *R.* 'Canary Bird' are light, neat and quite graceful. In the same way the rounded thicket of *R.farrerii* has scaled-down leaves. The pinky-purple foliage of *R.rubrifolia* has more or less of a grey bloom that enhances the overall delicacy.

Hazels, elders, buddlejas and other energetic shrubs will have been dealt with by the surgeon-gardener in the winter and come the spring they shoot into activity. The hazels and elders are ready to produce mammoth-sized pristine leaves. The sumachs, too, may be cut back hard to encourage outstanding foliage. *Rhus glabra, R.osbeckii* and *R.typhina* will all respond magnificently. Other trees and shrubs respond to being cut back; particularly impressive are *Ailanthus glandulosa* and *Paulownia tomentosa*.

Trees in early leaf can be spectacular. Whitebeams with leaf buds breaking and young leaves unfurling look as though they are decorated overall with very special candles. As they expand the picture fills out so that the tree begins to look like a silver cloud. *Sorbus aria* is fine, but there are varieties even more splendid. *S.a.magnifica* will end up with much the largest leaves of any. Some of the tree acers combine the unwrapping of their infant leaves with bright bracted limy flowers. The very popular *A. negundo* 'Variegatum' is easy, wonderful in spring and an attractive well-formed tree through the year with boldly lobed variegated leaves. The young leaves of some trees join with stem colour to provide the full picture. The hanging curtain of yellow produced by the golden weeping willow stems seems to take on a new sheen when the buds break and golden green leaves begin to grow.

Sumer is Icumen in

'Lhude sing cuccu!
Groweth sed and bloweth med
And sprongeth the wode nu.
Sing cuccu!'

With the summer and the loud cuckoo comes the splendour of the clothed tree and bush. Herbaceous plants can be as fulfilled foliarly but some will be more occupied with their flowers. Whilst many shrubs and trees outgrow their early polished spring newness, others continue to make new foliage alongside the maturer leaves. Rather than an overall steady effort, some appear to have two main surges of activity, one in spring and another in summer. A ground-covering favourite of mine is the bramble, *Rubus tricolor.* It keeps near the soil with unshaven stems covered with chestnut honey-coloured stubble and simple leaves embossed and polished dark green to look freshly minted at all times. It has the advantage of being more or less evergreen and is a most effective ground cover. In quite a different vein the eucalypts retain a good-as-new appearance throughout their evergreen life.

Contrasting foliage of (centre) day-lily *(Hemerocallis)*, hosta (front), and fern *(Dryopteris filix-mas)*

Many trees and shrubs grown for their unusual leaf colour become more effective as the leaf mass swells through the spring and into summer. The low dark clouds of purple red held to earth by *Cotinus* 'Royal Purple' or one of its kin are dramatic throughout the summer, when the higher held masses of golden *Robinia pseudoacacia* 'Frisia' improve. Others lose some of their early promise, the golden Indian bean, *Catalpa bignonioides* 'Aurea', becomes a shade greener but a little loss of brilliance scarcely matters as the colour is still soft and glowing whilst the leaf size is theatrical. Come the autumn all leaves become golden.

Silvery-leaved shrubs and plants can often improve through the late spring and summer. Those that, like *Senecio* 'Sunshine', retain their foliage through the winter may become grey and more sombre looking in the dark months. By then rain and time have reduced the effectiveness of the short silky hairs that give the silvered appearance. New leaves have glistening silken down.

Herbaceous plants, grown as much or more for their foliage as for any floral frivolity, get underway in spring but come into their own later; the dark-polished leaves of acanthus come boldly cut, almost like scrolls. Some forms are more intricately serrated than a large

OPPOSITE
The bold-leaved vine *Vitis coignettiae*, which can have leaves up to 30cm (1ft) long and across. The foliage turns many brilliant colours in the autumn *(Author)*

cross-cut saw. Others are silver veined. All are splendid and a foil for the paler-leaved silver wormwood, the lemon balm or the pale-green tiarellas. The thalictrums with steel- or silver-grey foliage, cut rather to the pattern of the maidenhair ferns, come almost rampantly onto the summer scene. *T. adiantifolium*, sometimes known as the hardy maidenhair, is more correctly *T. minus* and is capable of being somewhat invasive, though its foliage is so pleasing that where space is not at a premium it may be given its head. Heavier calibre *T. speciosissimum* can reach much higher and is very impressive with notably glaucous foliage and not unpleasing primrose heads of small flowers gathered together like many small powder puffs. It is not invasive. The glorious succulent upright two metre — six to eight feet — stems of *Macleaya microcarpa* 'Coral Plume' are magnificently clothed with their unique wide cordate leaves. The whole plant is redolent of vigour, even in poor soils it will run riot and a near forest of stems appear where the previous year there were but one or two.

Ferns

Ferns take their time starting in uncertain early spring weather, but few plants are more fascinating to watch break their winter dormancy. There are thousands to choose from. By summer one of the easiest to grow, the shuttlecock fern, *Matteuccia struthiopteris,* has fully expanded so that one can look down into the shuttlecock form and marvel at the exact intricacy of design. The black runners that

The silver-grey dwarf willow *Salix lanata*, with the spring foliage of *Iris pseudacoris* 'Variegata' and the prostrate juniper *J. sabina* 'Tamariscifolia' *(Author)*

slide out just under the soil surface ensure that, where there was one there will soon be many — a shuttlecock factory. The furry brown infant fronds of *Gymnocarpium dryopteris,* the oak fern, roll back like a controlled yo-yo and the firm fresh lacework of mature leaves points away from the central growing point. The extraordinary variety of hardy ferns can inveigle one into a lifetime's study. Of all the specification details, the basic one of size gives a scale of variation from tiny species such as the neat little wallrue and common spleenwort, often found like lizards clinging to walls, up to the giant royal fern, *Osmunda regalis*, growing in a lush spot and reaching perhaps 2.5 to 3m (8 to 10ft) high (at Tresco Abbey in the Scillies specimens grow to 4.5m (15ft) in height).

Some shrubs are a little ordinary in leaf but are likely to be included in a planting scheme because their floral donation is so generous, timely, or well loved. The early blaze of forsythias may be enjoyed over the neighbour's fence or in municipal plantings, but few can resist tucking in one or two and then by midsummer the leaf mass is scarcely spectacular — the best that may be said of it is that it is green and healthy. Rather the same may be written of hybrid lilacs although the species are often lighter and more graceful. How should these be handled? Possibly they could be planted behind more favoured shrubs where they will be seen while in flower but where the surrounding shrubs, if picked for their good contrasting foliage, will be the focus of attention in subsequent months. Purple-red leaved *Cotinus coggygria* 'Royal Purple', silver eucalypt, golden elder, variegated weigelas are obvious candidates for such a line up.

The herbaceous array is in full flower and foliage by midsummer. Hostas in huge variety, whilst splendid in moist soils and maybe best with some shade, will grow with rapidity and hardiness even in spots that are not very favourable. Roots reach deep and wide to support the sculptured leaf masses. The flowers are of secondary interest but can still be pleasant.

Other plants worth growing for their foliage alone are more generous with flower; the astilbes will persist in dryish soils but here their performance is definitely below par; they will respond to a damp soil by producing a thick ground cover of healthy, shining foliage. The flower plumes, white, pink or red, are held above the foliage and even in old age contrast charmingly with the leafy background. Rather like an astilbe writ large, *Artemisia lactiflora* produces a mass of deeply cut narrowly pointed green foliage. It needs placing where the soil does not dry out. The high airy plumes (1.2–1.5m/4–5ft) of creamy small flowers are pleasing but not dramatic. The disposition to enjoy moisture is in contrast to its silver-leaved relations that flourish best in dryish situations. *Aruncus sylvester* will enjoy a similar damp soil and has neat, but pinnate foliage not dissimilar to that of the astilbes but it can make a wide rounded mass about a metre — some three or four feet high. Above this it will extend many showy creamy intricate plumes to reach nearly two metres — perhaps six foot — high in June. Equally tall are the yellow spires of *Ligularia przewalskii* with huge, dark, basically heart-shaped leaves but strongly serrated.

In the background of the border *Macleaya cordata* or *M. micro-carpa* may romp away. It has been mentioned already. Just a word here to suggest that any invasive tendency can easily be checked by hoeing through the extending runners. Where it can be given its head, it can be magnificent. Especially fine against a dark background, the pale stems and somewhat bronzed leaves are most attractive. They are held more or less horizontally, their basic round shape being cut into in the manner of the rounded interlocking shapes of jigsaw pieces. It is one of the finest herbaceous foliage plants; the spikes of flowers give a creamy effect in *M. cordata* and a pinky coffee shade with *M. microcarpa* in the usually grown form, 'Coral Plume'.

Herbaceous plants of lesser stature range from the vividly silver-white cut-leaved artemesias, the very cut fresh-green ferny foliage of the smaller *Adonis vernalis,* to the rounded, notched, glaucous leaves of the flower-arranger's standby, *Alchemilla mollis* frothing with sulphur flower sprays, the leaves often holding jewel-like globules of water in their centres. More pointed, almost ivy leaved, is *Tiarella cordifolia* with pleasing soft leaves of golden green but often interestingly marked with brown shading. It grows and spreads easily. Rather more dainty are the epimediums that are now widely grown as ground-cover plants, the flat, clean-cut heart-shaped leaves held more or less on a horizontal plane by almost thread-thin stems. The wonder is that so narrow a stem can do the

Maroon-flushed foliage of British wildling *Euphorbia amygdaloides* (back), and one of the lungworts *Pulmonaria saccharata*

job. The leaves are a basic green enriched with bronze and red patterning. Fresh paler-green ones are produced through the summer so that an interesting picture in colour tone, and leaf shape is built up.

One could wax euphoric about the euphorbias, they are very varied. We have native ones that can be a nuisance as weeds. Some, like *E. characias wulfenii* can almost qualify as shrubs, with their neat grey-green foliage and large sulphur-green rounded flower heads. *E. griffithii*, now usually seen in the 'Fireflow' form, extends its range with underground suckers and in the open air makes mounds of neat foliage with some pinky-red colouring pencilled around the edges of the new leaves and flame coloured, wide flower heads. *E. myrsinites* makes a low silver-blue widening mound that remains bright throughout the year and is covered with lime-yellow flowers in spring.

Playing a rather similar role the resting rootstocks of *Sedum spectabile* quickly move into growth in the spring and by summer are large, succulent-leaved masses of silver grey and green that are later topped with wide heads of dark pink-red flowers, a frequent stopping place for butterflies. The stems can be left through the winter,

Senecio 'Sunshine', shining bright with midsummer flowers, next to the grass *Hakonechloa macra variegata* 'Aureola', almost as bright. At the rear is the *Hydrangea paniculata* 'Grandiflora' *(Cloudesley Rd, London)*

in shape and dark-brown colour they help to lessen the winter's dominance.

Autumn Glory

The chemical changes that take place within the leaf to reduce green to yellow, oranges, and reds are influenced by many factors and fine autumnal colours can follow weather that might have been thought inimical to their production. Too dry a late summer and autumn can sometimes minimise the autumn display.

Pilgrimages are made to gardens featuring autumn colouring. The arboretum at Westonbirt in Gloucestershire is a popular outing when the summer ends. Here the acers lead the display. On the way to Westonbirt the hedgerows can be lit up with the oranges and reds of the wild maple, *A. campestre*. This is a very nice, neat tree and worth a place in the larger garden. The most popular of garden species is, of course, *A. palmatum* in its many manifestations. Nearly 150 forms are available in Britain. The two most obvious variable characteristics are leaf colour and form. From pale-cream and peach shades, the colours singly or two or three suffused together cover yellow, greens, pinks, oranges, reds, and purples. The basic leaf is

The opulent large-leaved Indian bean tree *Catalpa bignoides* 'Aurea' dominates this well-balanced group. The long strap-leaved *Agapanthus* in full bloom adds contrasting colour whilst the clipped golden conifer adds to the brightness. Blue-grey rue *Ruta graveolens* is neat below. Variegated *Weigela florida* 'Aureovariegata' (right) is one of the easiest bright-leaved shrubs *(Coates Manor)*

rounded but lobed, this lobing being more deeply cut into some, whilst being so exaggerated in others that the main veins of the leaf are scarcely more than outlined by leaf tissue, giving a filigree effect. Autumn colours are golds, oranges and reds. *Acer griseum* is a species whose flaking bark is very decorative, its foliage in autumn is kindled to become flaming colours. *A. nikoense, A. cissifolium,* and *A. henryi* are quite closely related to *A. griseum* and all act out brilliant swansong behaviour before winter dormancy. The very robust Norway maple, *A. platanoides,* makes a large tree and dies off colourfully. There are various named forms, *A.p.* 'Crimson King' is possibly the darkest purple red of all large-leaved trees.

Large-scale colour pictures can be created by several oaks such as *Quercus coccinea, Q. heterophylla* and *Q. palustris.* The tulip tree, *Liriodendron tulipifera,* will take many years to become a giant, which may be just as well in any but really large gardens, but young specimens are attractive with their unusually shaped leaves and their autumn golds. The fastigiate form can be accommodated rather more easily.

There are few more wholesale stunning effects in the garden than those made by the climbing vines. The true Virginia creeper, *Parthenocissus quinquefolia,* is glorious in its autumn regalia. *P. henryana* is as lovely, whilst the very popular *P. tricuspidata* is probably the richest coloured of all. Many true vines are beautifully coloured before leaf fall. The largest leaved, *Vitis coignetiae,* can be spectacular in many flaming colours as it covers walls, pergolas, carports, sheds, or hanging in great curtains from its natural home in supporting trees.

Rather more shrub-sized shrubs can be highly decorative through the autumn pageant. Many deciduous berberis species and hybrids become incandescent, as do also some viburnums and the spindleberries that have their lovely fruits accompanying the turning foliage. All the *Rhus* species flare into burning reds and oranges to make their positions a focal point at a time when there is plenty of competition. Then suddenly their leaves are gone.

On the whole the herbaceous plants are less given to showy autumn display; they fade and fail with varying degrees of decorum. The dahlias, all shiny vigour one day are black the next following a frost. Hostas become yellow or pale gold and for a short while are pleasing before they collapse. Paeonies can turn a reasonable golden colour but most herbaceous plants are undistinguished in their departure. It is a relief to tidy up after they have finished.

Winter Stalwarts

As winter returns we are left with the more-or-less bare bones of the garden. True there are important crops of berries, some to feed the birds and others apparently not to their taste. These scarcely distract us from our view of the winter garden and at no other season do we realise the importance of sensible design. It need not be complicated. It does mean remembering when planting that the deciduous drop their leaves and though pleasing in outline they may do little to dispel winter's gloom. Coloured stem and bark may help but now the evergreens take over.

In some gardens considerable collections of conifers dominate the design throughout the year, but even here in winter they look somewhat different during the darker months. First, the eye is not distracted by the colour of herbaceous or deciduous things, then the lighting arrangements of winter are less brilliant. Finally, conifers and evergreens are not unchanging. Many golden conifers can acquire quite distinctly bronzy suffusions, some green ones become more blue or purple toned. The flat metallic leaves of many eucalypts can become darker and enriched with pinky-purple shading. Hollies that have grown well through the summer may not appear to change a lot but new foliage becomes rather darker, and variegated forms can often become more striking, the contrast of colours being more accentuated.

We sing of the holly and the ivy. A collection of ivies can be quite dramatically different in autumn and winter. The usual wild forms may change a little but some of the more usual ones, particularly the variegated types, can take on a variety of pink, mauve, purple and bronze colourings.

Whilst winter-flowering heathers make invaluable floral contributions, others make almost as lively an impact by their leaf colours. In the active growing months the *Erica cinerea* series selected for their golden foliage may be somewhat bronzed but the winter tends to make the colouring more definite. The first frosts help infuse the bright gold with greater quantities of red, orange and bronze. In the distance one may wonder what can be blooming so freely at this time of year, eyes focussing on the heathers realise the mistake.

We need colour close to house and garden entrance in these winter months. Focal points can be made or enhanced by winter form and colour that may be seen from the house and the areas most frequently traversed in winter. More distant spots will not need such close attention. Bright heathers are wonderful investments. Several dwarf conifers can lend colour, form, and character.

In the middle distance an unmixed rose bed or herbaceous border can become a dull area for months unless something is done to preserve some form and colour. Garden ornaments and statuary may help together with walls and paths. In the herbaceous border discourage wholesale tidying; with some selection the dried flowerheads of dwarf michaelmas daisies or the flat panicles of *Sedum spectabile* together with bleached grasses and others can lend shape and muted colour not to be despised. A relatively few shrubs or trees can help to maintain interest where otherwise a flat formless site is threatened.

Evergreen berberis, mahonias, viburnums will flourish in most places. Where lime is not present rhododendrons and camellias come into their own with kalmias and pieris forms. Hollies both plain and variegated are excellent value in most soils, proof against the worst of the weather. Plant some unusual forms to give addi-

tional interest. Conifers are valued as much for their form and mass
as for their colours. Their greens are various; the golden forms may
be uniformly so or may be basically green but yellow at the growing
points. Obviously yellow and gold will brighten the winter scene
but a golden bonanza can look almost tawdry. One or two carefully
placed golden ones can be most welcome.

Other evergreens may be brought into play. The gold and silver
variegated elaeagnus forms can be as bright in colour as flowers.
They certainly stand up well to the winter weather. *E.pungens*
'Aureo Variegata' can be one of the brightest spots in the winter
garden. Even golden privet should not be ignored. It will retain
most of its leaves through the worst of the winter. The spotted
aucubas were popular with the Victorians and a well-formed bush
can do much to brighten the bleakness of winter. *Eucalyptus
gunnii* and *E.niphophila* will gleam silver and grey, almost as
bright as in midsummer.

A garden full of variegated plants would look artificial, everything
painted and gilded; however, a few well-displayed evergreen ones
can be invaluable. The trees and shrubs will be obvious, but more
lowly things, such as the vigorous large golden-leaved ivy, *Hedera
colchica* 'Dentata Variegata', can be almost as important. It looks
lively in all seasons. *Yucca filamentosa* in dark green can be a useful

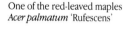

One of the red-leaved maples
Acer palmatum 'Rufescens'

Hardy *Yucca filamentosa* with lavender and spotted-leaved *Pulmonaria* which has gathered lots of common names on account of its leaves or flowers of pink and blue, eg 'spotted dog' and 'soldiers and sailors'

bit of hardy living sculpture, and if you can provide a well-drained spot in the south or west *Y.gloriosa* may also be tried. The long narrow stiff leaves are armour tipped and impressive at all times. There is, too, *Y.g.*'Variegata' with yellow striped leaves.

At a more herbaceous level the variegated periwinkles both gold and silver forms are winter bright; they are easy to grow and very useful.

Ilex aquifolium 'Argentea Marginata', one of the most popular and effective variegated hollies (female) *(Author)*

4   The Evergreen Evergold etc

We need another word to describe non-deciduous plants. They may or may not be green. In a climate in which many deciduous plants can have lost their foliage before the end of October and are not re-clothed until April, their winter is virtually half the year. Regardless of the calendar, winter is easily the longest season. This makes the role of 'evergreens' crucially important.

First we think of conifers, then of hollies and other larger shrubs and trees. The few evergreen climbers are important. They include legions of ivies. Smaller gardens have made dwarf conifers popular, and in those gardens heathers are now being appreciated for the colours of their foliage. New kinds of conifers and heathers are introduced each year.

A Return to Victorian Values

Victorians took evergreen plants seriously. Their shubberies were filled with impressive collections, some, examples of the topiarist's art, others free growing. The backbone of these collections were the privets, laurels, spotted aucubas and ivies grown as shrubs; rhododendrons and many other newly discovered plants were also pressed into service.

It was an age of many enthusiasms; the craze for ferns was one of the most important horticultural ones. These were grown outside and later, as industrial pollution became worse and affected the ferns, they were grown under glass. Many were evergreens. Fern fanciers combed the countryside to find new variations of the fifty species wild in Britain. More than three hundred variants were named of each of the soft shield fern, *Polystichum setiferum* and the lady fern, *Athyrium filix-femina.* Most of these were lost during World War I. Vegetables took the place of ferns. Knowledgeable gardeners joined the army and those who survived returned to a world that did not favour the maintenance of large fern collections.

There are signs of a revival of interest in hardy ferns; this is scarcely surprising. They are beautiful and easy to grow. Air is far cleaner and ferns respond to this. Much of the lesser garden space is shaded; many city gardens rarely see direct sunshine. Ferns enjoy shade and thrive in awkward spots where little else will flourish. The hart's tongue, *Asplenium scolopendrium,* the broad buckler fern, *Dryopteris dilatata,* and the soft shield fern, *Polystichum setiferum,* and their many varieties provide a treasure trove of evergreen types. The three little ferns commonly found growing in the mortar of old walls are all evergreens that can be grown in similar sites in the garden or in the rock garden. These are the maidenhair spleenwort, the wallrue, and the rustyback fern. The common polypody that creeps over mossy rocks and tree trunks is a larger free ranger.

Contrasting foliage of (back) *Fatsia japonica* (often used as a pot plant but perfectly hardy), the fern *Dryopteris affinis grandiceps* 'Askew', and (front) *Tiarella cordifolia*, sometimes called foam flower because of its sprays of small creamy flowers

Conifers

Colours in conifers veer from the lemon gold of the small-leaved dense columns of the *Cupressus macrocarpa* 'Goldcrest' to the silvery blue of kinds like *Chamaecyparis lawsoniana* 'Pembury Blue' and the very dark black green of some of the yews. Many are more or less bicoloured, gold and green, cream and green, or with interesting shades of brown or purple. Many conifers maintain more or less the same colouring year-round, but others mark the seasons. Flowering adds interest and a little colour. Conifers are not painted in one completely colourfast shade; some thujas can change dramatically.

Often colours are the result of light playing on the surfaces of the leaves as well as the underlying pigmentation. Waxy surfaces wear over the year and new shades appear. As leaves age their metabolism changes and colours of leaf surfaces change also. Many conifers display one colour at the growing points and another behind in their older recesses. This certainly applies to many of the *Chamaecyparis lawsoniana* varieties. Overall effects depend heavily on the growing tips. Two- or three-toned patterns of green, or golds and greens, are established, patterns whose relative balances vary through the year. Needle sizes, and the way they are held, catch the light in different ways and produce quite distinct effects. Basic colours of two conifers may be exactly the same examined inside, but growing outside the result is totally different. Polished surfaces of some give a more lively effect than others, like yews with rich

OPPOSITE
Dwarf conifers *Thuja orientalis* 'Aurea Nana' (one of the brightest of all), *T.occidentalis* 'Sunkist' (right), and the prostrate golden yew, *Taxus baccata* 'Adpressa Aurea' *(Eastgrove Cottage Garden Nursery)*

tones having an impressive brooding darkness.

The impact of conifers in our plans depends on many factors, chief of which is the quantity planted and the proportion that these represent of the total of garden trees and shrubs. Specimen size is another factor. In a suburban garden that I pass frequently, a lot of smaller conifers are planted. Most of these are from 45cm to 1.8m (18in to 6ft) high. Well-kept lawns and the conifers are the dominant features of the garden plan. It is surprising how pleasing and lively it looks, never more so than in winter when neighbouring gardens have a noticeably vacant appearance.

Most gardeners are inveterate collectors who enjoy experimenting with a variety of new plants. Too many conifers might restrict the building up of their polyglot choice, but gardeners will still want them for twelve-month architectural and sculptural strength. Several good-sized conifers can form the backbone of the garden design. Pyramidal forms bring the sky into the picture. Junipers like 'Skyrocket' can act the part that some of the narrow cypresses do in French, Italian and other Mediterranean gardens.

Other low junipers hug the ground. The deservedly popular *Juniperus chinensis* 'Pfitzeriana Aurea' is particularly effective with

Juniperus x 'Pfitzeriana Aurea' contrasted with the interesting intergeneric hybrid x *Fatshedera lizei*, bred from *Fatsia japonica* and *Hedera helix* 'Hibernica' *(Denmans)*

sweeping wide well-furnished branches pointing out and slightly upwards. One can cover several square metres with layers of branches building up to a modest .75m (2ft) height. Whilst a prostrate conifer can grow rapidly, an even more immediate dramatic impact is made by planting three youngsters in a triangle about 45 or 60cm (18in or 2ft) apart. They soon meet and look one. Of course upright conifers can be bulked up by planting three or more saplings in a group but the situation is different because two of the three would need to be removed before they merge so that one unspoilt mature specimen is eventually left.

Some upright conifers grow very rapidly, the hedging leylandiis can grow 45 to 60cm (18in to 2ft) a year even in their youth. Others like *Chamaecyparis lawsoniana* 'Pembury Blue' grow steadily rather than spectacularly. Ideas about the rates of growth are often erratic. Yew is thought of as tediously slow, possibly a reflection of the knowledge that churchyard specimens may be several hundreds of years old. However the yew in youth is upwardly mobile in a satisfyingly energetic manner.

Hedges — Coniferous and Others

Garden hedges used as boundary walls or as dividing partitions, may be deciduous or evergreen. Evergreens are more popular. Deciduous beech hedges are induced by close clipping to retain browned dead autumn leaves for much, if not all, of the winter. Where laurel and privet reigned supreme in smaller gardens in the past, the

There was once a vogue for using the green type of *Lonicera nitida* as a hedging plant and it can be so used for smaller interior hedges and topiary. *Lonicera nitida* 'Baggessen's Gold' with its bright colour is useful in many spots that need lightening

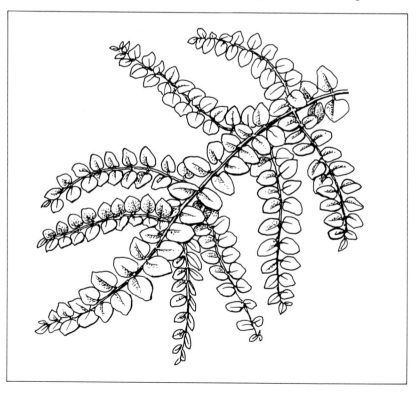

leylandiis have almost a monopoly. In larger, older gardens holly and yew are the large hedging plants. The relative slowness of holly in its early years has not helped its suburban popularity.

Several conifer species have been tried as hedging plants. Most are non-starters as they do not readily produce fresh growth behind any pruned wood. Species that respond to the knife include *Chamaecyparis lawsoniana, C.nootkatensis, Cupressus macrocarpa, Thuja occidentalis* and *T.plicata*. The *C. x leylandii* hybrids are the result of the mating of *C.macrocarpa* and *C.nootkatensis. C.macrocarpa* was much in vogue in the twenties, thirties and forties but, whilst a rapid grower producing a dense neat hedge in its juvenile leaf form, it tended to outgrow its required dimensions becoming top heavy for its relatively underdeveloped root system. It was also liable to have parts or even complete trees die, so leaving awkward gaps. *C.nootkatensis* offers no real advantage over its very versatile leylandii offspring. *C. lawsoniana,* on the other hand, in its many forms and colours can make an elegant hedge. Its good points can be listed. Provided it is kept well groomed it will produce rich evergreen colour to soil level. It makes fresh growth after pruning. It is very hardy. It grows reasonably fast, but not like Jack's beanstalk, so less pruning is required than with leylandiis. There is a cloned kind called *C.l.* 'Green Hedger' specifically grown in the nursery trade for hedgeing work. Of the two thujas, *T.plicata* is the better, but it has no special merits not possessed by *C. lawsoniana* or *C. x leylandii.*

'Castlewellan' is the golden-green leylandii that helps to bring a lighter brighter tone to the garden but, if used exclusively, can perhaps be a little brash.

The advantages of the leylandiis are these. They are comparatively cheap. They grow more quickly than other evergreens. If tended properly they provide dense cover from head to toe. Colours are clean and do not tarnish in the winter. Their energy, so welcome in many ways, is also a disadvantage. The equation is, Energy=Work. The more energetic the hedge, the more work that is demanded of the gardener to keep it within acceptable bounds.

Holly Hedges
It would be difficult to argue that any form of hedge is better than one well made of holly. Initially more expensive to plant, and in the first year or two slow, but good cultivation can develop a reasonable hedge quite quickly. It could be more permanent than many a wall, and can be grown perhaps three metres — ten or more feet high to make the most effective of all windbreaks. It will certainly make a stock- and child-proof barrier. Dark-blue blacks, dark greens, and variegated shades are rich and healthy. Once established they grow steadily but can be kept under control moderately easily by an annual trim towards the end of the summer.

Hedges can be grown to almost any height and provide a good backcloth for a plant such as 'Miss Willmott's ghost,' *Eryngium giganteum,* or some of the tall thistles. Hedge quality is going to depend initially on planting good stock in well-prepared soil in the spring, and using specimens that branch low to the ground. Plants should be encouraged to produce plenty of low growth and, as the hedge takes shape, the faces should slope back as it grows upwards. In three or four years the hedge should be well started and then can be maintained for a century or two.

Yew Hedges

Yew grows more quickly than holly. It also makes a first-class, dark, weatherproof hedge. For most gardeners the polish of the larger decorative holly leaves gives it the edge over the yew but the yew's matt finish and rich dark colour is very effective. Plants are exceedingly strong growing and a mass of roots will mean that little of importance can be grown close to the hedge. The colour marvellously highlights plants like delphiniums, foxtail lilies, or silver-leaved *Cytisus battandieri* or eucalyptus species.

Eucalyptus

Of approximately six hundred eucalyptus species in Australia, those growing well in temperate climates while limited are more than is commonly supposed. Tasmania is closer to our lines of latitude and many of its eucalyptus species experience winter cold. Some species are almost surefire successes; others may be equally worth trying. Seeds of more than fifty varieties are available in Britain; some species grown from seed may result in head-high specimens

Box and yew hedges, rich-coloured living walls
(Author)

in one season. A few packets of seed cost little and the results could be surprising. Conifers can provide pyramids or pointed columns of dark colour; the eucalypts are likely to give attractively marked trunks with showers of silver-grey foliage in light clouds overhead. It is an interesting contrast of styles.

Eucalyptus gunnii is the most popular because of its hardiness and shining rounded silvery juvenile foliage tightly clasped round every young twig. Flower arrangers love it. Adult leaves are flat, pointed and spear-shaped of silver grey. Even more winterproof is *E.niphophila,* a slightly variable but always lovely tree with branches often steely white and hung with long, flat, pointed leaves of metal grey that flash in the light.

Native evergreen trees and shrubs are few. The evergreens in our gardens are likely to have come from parts where the climate is more equable and moisture constantly available. Probably the only genuine native evergreen trees are the Scots pine and the holly, though box and common juniper can reach tree-like proportions. The strawberry tree, *Arbutus unedo*, gets as near as the southwest of Ireland and will usually do well in Britain but it takes time to reach tree stature. Evergreens are at risk in exposed areas where there is considerable wind and cold. Wind will try to desiccate the leaves. Where dry conditions and wind combine the damage is greatest. Evergreen oaks were badly affected by the recent bad winters, the searing winds doing as much damage as the continued freezing cold. But oaks are trees of parkland or very large gardens.

Modest-sized gardens are not without special trees. *Magnolia grandiflora* will grow happily against the house walls with 'grandi' leaves as well as flowers. *Arbutus menziesii* will eventually make a tree and this, like the magnolia, benefits from the more favourable microclimate of the domestic garden. Cloud-shaped masses of the arbutus can make a big impact, the leaves being large and polished make a dark background for the upright pyramidal panicles of creamy-white, heather-type flowers.

Shrubby Evergreens
Whilst evergreen trees can almost be counted on one's fingers, evergreen shrubs in numerous shapes and sizes can be relied on to retain healthy foliage year-long. Many genera with deciduous members, like the berberises, the cotoneasters, and viburnums, have important evergreen species. Other genera like the rhododendrons, the heathers and their relatives, the pieris, are evergreen.

The shrubs are dealt with later but here are a few points. The uninitiated would probably not consider rhododendrons foliage plants. This could be because of dullish *R.ponticum* which has escaped into the wild where it swamps wide areas and smothers native plants. Common hybrids like 'Pink Pearl' are better controlled but their foliage is pedestrian rather than exciting like other species and their hybrids. New foliage of some can be a joy. Many species have highly polished leaves, but others are rough and some appear almost to be encrusted. While the upper surfaces are what one notices first, an examination of the lower surfaces of many will discover lovely coverings of golden, rusty or chocolate-coloured felts or waxy whites.

The variation in size of the rhododendron leaves parallels the differing size of plants. Some are young trees with leaves 25 to 30cm (10in to 1ft) long, others are miniatures with tiny leaves and resembling natural bonsai specimens.

The cotoneasters have dark clean-cut leaves, more-or-less polished, and neatly held. Branching methods distinguish these, rather than the oval pointed leaves that are workmanlike and respectable. The herringbone pattern of *C.horizontalis* is very stylised; a few other species approach this style. Others have wide-ranging long-reaching branches like those of *C.franchetii*. The larger types like *C. x watererii* after attaining formidable stature have side, arching branches that fall somewhat downwards; one or two are completely pendulous.

Some cotoneasters are evergreen, some are deciduous, others do not decide which until the winter weather arrives. If the winter is mild many like *C.horizontalis* will keep most leaves until the new flush arrives with the spring, but if it gets too inclement they shrug off their foliage and are decorative by means of branches and berries. The ground huggers, such as *C.dammerii* and the fine hybrids can cover acres of awkward ground, but in winter the dark-green leaves are mixed with a proportion of older ones coloured orange or red.

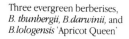

Three evergreen berberises, *B. thunbergii, B.darwinii,* and *B.lologensis* 'Apricot Queen'

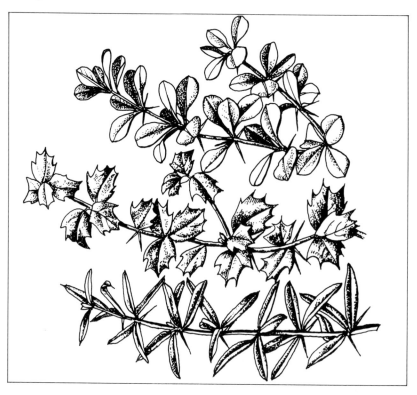

Viburnums with evergreen foliage are led by the most frequently seen, *V. laurustinus* (known since its Victorian heyday as tinus). Its rounded masses of dark oval leaves build up to a height of more than two metres — eight or more feet — and are well decorated with posies of pinky-white flowers in the winter months. The foliage of *V. davidii* is distinctive with larger leaves than *V. laurustinus,* and with the embossed veins being unusual in running longitudinally. The polish of the surfaces and the red leaf stalks add distinction to a wide, low-spreading shrub.

Now for the thorny problem of the berberis family. Relatively few of these grow in private gardens although large numbers of some species are planted in places like motorway service stations and public parks where plants need to be hard-wearing. Berberises are strong on self-protection, being armed with thorns and spiny foliage. In the wild, most are somewhat variable plants causing confusion because of their readiness to cross-pollinate.

The most popular evergreen berberis is itself a hybrid, *B. x stenophylla,* the offspring of *B. darwinii,* and *B. empetrifolia.* The child is more graceful than either of the attractive parents and hardier than *B. darwinii.* It can be used as a specimen in the border or in solitary splendour in the lawn making a strong focal point. Its dense mass is made up of countless slender upright stems from which graceful arching branches emerge, bearing prolific small, rich, tangerine-gold flowers. Standing 2 to 3.5m (5 to 10ft) and the same dimension in width, it can be an important statuesque clump in the garden whether in or out of bloom.

The berberis genus has not attracted great popularity; a berberis society has yet to be formed, but they are useful-sized shrubs for the modern garden and are trouble free. Many are neat, but others such as *B. hakeoides* can grow strongly and untidily; nevertheless this species has handsome and very unusual foliage, as well as pleasing spring blossom. Planted in the right spot the rather gawky manner can be screened by tidier plants.

Closely related to the berberises and once submerged within the same genus are the mahonias. Of course it is excusable to say 'no garden should be without them'. This cliché is justified by the fine year-round foliage of some species and hybrids as well as the generous supply of bloom proffered by many in the worst months. *M. bealei* and *M. japonica* are the two hardiest of winter-flowering species but a series of hybrids, *M. x media,* between *M. japonica* and the beautiful but more tender *M. lomariifolia* have become most popular. 'Charity', 'Buckland', 'Lionel Fortescue', and 'Winter Sun' are four named ones, 'Charity' being the most widespread. The pinnate foliage, like pale holly leaves ironed almost flat, looks splendid at all times with that touch of class denied to *M. aquifolium.*

However forget class, *M. aquifolium* can survive in the most awkward of spots where there may be only scant soil. Strong suckers will reach into unpromising places and new stems appear. It forms wide stands of upright stems. Foliage is tough, polished, and rich green often suffused with purple, becoming red in the autumn.

Rubus tricolor is one of the most energetic of ground-cover plants. Polished dark leaves with impressed venation are attractive, but its low sprinting branches root as they go and can cover wide areas, so it must be introduced only where such behaviour is acceptable

Robust, quick, and handsome cover is made by *Rubus tricolor,* of the blackberry family but mercifully without thorns. Rich, green, embossed leaves horizontally held from brown-bristled stems allow no soil to show and keep all seeding weeds at bay.

House walls can be completely clothed with ivies or other climbers. Of these more later. The warmth of the walls encourages shrubs that would be unhappy in the open, in some parts shrubs like camellias can be helped by this protection and will repay thoughtfulness with well-mannered growth and clean-cut, polished, uniform foliage. The evergreen climber, *Clematis armandii,* in one of its forms may disguise a fallpipe as it reaches towards the bedroom window. It is a shame more use is not made of house walls. The marriage of garden and house can lend greater distinction to both.

In planning and planting the evergreen contingent in the garden think first of hardiness, size, mass, form, colours and textures. Assess character and select only the best of each type, the most appropriate for the garden conditions and the overall plan. Consider including clumps of bamboos, dramatically weeping conifers such as *Chamaecyparis nootkatensis* 'Pendula', large-leaved Indian bean trees or, on a smaller scale, some of the very stylised miniature shrubby ivies, the more unusually formed hollies or butcher's broom. This last has leaf-like structures that are free of any obligation to drop in the autumn or at any time as, whilst labouring as leaves, they are really flattened portions of stem.

Some plants highly regarded as house plants are perfectly hardy. Two very dissimilar ones are *Fatsia japonica* and *Tolmiea menziesii.* The last is the amusing little piggy-back plant, in its penny plain or tuppence variegated form. It thrives on thousands of kitchen window sills throughout the land. It is difficult to resist the temptation to grow more from the plantlets appearing where full-sized leaves join their stalks. The hairy, light-green maple-shaped leaves are soft and pleasing and when planted outdoors can nestle in corners of stone steps or towards the front of a border.

Fatsia japonica has been grown for well over a century as a garden shrub and house plant. It could well hold the record for having the largest leaves of any hardy evergreen plant. These can measure 30 to 45cm (12 to 18in) across. They are tough, rich green and polished, handsomely shaped with seven or nine pointed fingerlobes in a palmate form.

Herbaceous Evergreens?

The question mark signifies the somewhat paradoxical nature of the heading. The *RHS Dictionary* defines herbaceous plants as those that may be cut down each year and which will then grow up again the following one as good as new.

In the herbaceous border's heyday everything was cut down at the year's end. Some plants thought of as herbaceous cannot be subjected to indiscriminate scything regimes. Many hellebores are evergreen; flowering in the winter or early spring they maintain last season's foliage at least until new growth is well underway. Many euphorbias organise in a similar manner. Among these are some of the most useful of foliage plants. The steely green-greys and purple-suffused euphorbias can form very well-balanced plants. *Helleborus argutifolius (H.corsicus)* has some of the finest leaves of any plant.

All parts of the garden are served by evergreens. There are wonderful grasses that look fresh and bright every season. New Zealand flax species and hybrids are dramatic, as modernistically sculptural as agaves. Alpines, we tend to think, spend their winter leafless below thick blankets of snow, but many small rock-garden plants may be used in sink or troughs and are full of leafy life during winter. Collections of sempervivums and sedums are child's play to grow but are great value. Even *Ajuga reptans* the humble bugle of our fields is worth its space in one or more of its colour-leaved forms. Dark mahogany-purple flat mats of foliage can be contrasted with green and cream variegated kinds, or tricoloured ones in shades of green, cream and crimson pink.

There is an evergreen for every spot.

Fatsia japonica with large polished leaves, *Alchemilla mollis* with foamy mustard-coloured flowers, *Sedum spectabile* (right) and *Santolina chamaecyparis*, lavender cotton on top of the wall *(Author)*

5

The review of these garden trees, concentrating on their foliar appeal, will emphasise those suitable for the smaller garden. It is important to know their rates of growth, their ultimate sizes, their shapes, and habits good and bad as we attempt to assess the trees.

Large leaves are impressive; those of some exotic walnuts and oaks are splendid. Youngsters of these make considerable impact. Walnuts are surprisingly fast growing and, with their mammoth handsome leaves are highly decorative, though they will need to be felled before reaching maturity. The Indian bean tree, *Catalpa bignonioides,* the tulip tree, *Liriodendron tulipifera,* and the pocket-handkerchief tree, *Davidia involucrata,* are three other distinguished exotics. Tulip trees can grow over 35m (100ft) tall. The potential stature of the other two is unlikely to cause concern and the tulip tree has sported a fastigiate form much easier in small gardens. Some genera not normally associated with opulent foliage can surprise with the odd well-dressed species. Willows have *Salix magnifica* with leaves as splendid as a good magnolia.

The form of trees is probably their most important feature. At one extreme are the fastigiate ones with arms stretched rigidly upright and pressed together, at the other extreme are weeping kinds with branches dramatically downswept. Few trees can be more atmospheric than weeping willows. The list of weeping trees is longer

Tree forms:
1 Fastigiate
2 Columnare
3 Conical
4 Pyramidal
5 Weeping
6 Arching
7 Contorted

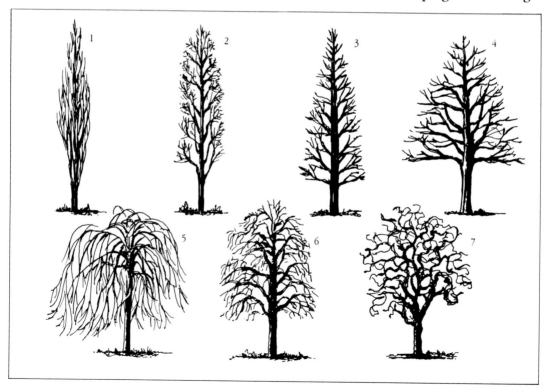

than that for fastigiates. Some weepers become very large trees. Smaller weepers are as stagey but of more manageable proportions.

Weeping Trees

		deciduous/ evergreen	ultimate height	
Abies alba 'Pendula'	Silver Fir	e	35m	(100ft)
Acer saccharinum 'Pendulum'		d	15m	(45ft)
Alnus incana 'Pendula'	Alder	d	10m	(30ft)
Betula pendula 'Youngii'	Birch	d	3m	(9-10ft)
p. 'Purpurea'		d	7m	(20ft)
Caragana arborescens 'Pendula'		d	3m	(9-10ft)
Carpinus betulus 'Pendula'	Hornbeam	e	12m	(35-40ft)
Cedrus atlantica 'Pendula'	Cedar	e	35m	(100ft)
Chamaecyparis lawsoniana 'Filifera'		e	17-25m	(50-80ft)
nootkatensis 'Pendula'		e	17-25m	(50-80ft)
Cornus florida 'Pendula'	Cornel	d	3m	(9-10ft)
Corylus avellana 'Pendula'	Hazel	d	3m	(9-10ft)
Cotoneaster multiflora		d	3-4m	(10-12ft)
Crataegus monogyna 'Pendula'	Hawthorn	d	3-4m	(10-12ft)
Fagus sylvatica 'Pendula'	Beech	d	5-7m	(15-20ft)
s.purpurea pendula		d	5-7m	(15-20ft)
Fraxinus angustifolia 'Pendula'	Ash	d	26m	(50ft)
excelsior 'Pendula'		d	20-30m	(60-90ft)
e. 'Wentworth'		d	15m	(50ft)
Genista aetnensis	Broom	d	5m	(15ft)
Ginkgo biloba 'Pendula'		e	17m	(50ft)
Ilex aquifolium 'Pendula'	Holly	e	3-7m	(10-20ft)
a. 'Argenteo Marginata Pendula'		e	3-7m	(10-20ft)
a. 'Aureo Pendula'		e	3-7m	(10-20ft)
Juglans regia 'Pendula'	Walnut	d	10-15m	(30-40ft)
Juniperus virginiana 'Pendula'	Juniper	e	6-10m	(20-30ft)
Laburnum anagyroides	Pendulum	d	5-7m	(15-20ft)
Larix pendula	Larch	d	12-17m	(40-50ft)
Malus prunifolia 'Pendula'	Crabapple	d	3-4m	(10-12ft)
'Cheals Weeping'		d	3-4m	(10-12ft)
'Red Jade'		d	3-4m	(10-12ft)
Morus alba 'Pendula'	Mulberry	d	4-7m	(12-20ft)
Populus tremula 'Pendula'	Aspen	d	7-10m	(20-30ft)
tremuloides 'Pendula'		d	8-10m	(20-30ft)
Prunus amygdalus 'Pendula'	Almond	d	5-7m	(15-20ft)
avium 'Pendula'	Gean	d	7m	(20ft)
mahaleb 'Pendula'	Cherry	d	7m	(20ft)
mume 'Pendula'	Japanese Apricot	d	3-5m	(10-15ft)
serotina 'Pendula'	Cherry	d	4-5m	(12-15ft)
Pyrus salicifolia 'Pendula'	Pear	d	4-5m	(12-15ft)
Quercus palustris 'Pendula'	Pin Oak	d	13-17m	(40-50ft)
pedunculata 'Pendula'	Oak	d	13-17m	(40-50ft)
Rhus cotinus 'Pendula'	Sumach	d	3-4m	(10-12ft)
Salix babylonica	Willow	d	13-17m	(40-50ft)
caprea 'Pendula'	Kilmarnock Willow	d	2-3m	(6-10ft)
purpurea 'Pendula'	Purple Weeping	d	3-4m	(8-12ft)
vitellina 'Pendula'	Golden Weeping	d	8-9m	(25-30ft)
Sambucus nigra 'Pendula'	Elder	d	3m	(10ft)
Sequoiadendron gigantea 'Pendulum'	Wellingtonia	e	18-22m	(55-70ft)
Sophora japonica 'Pendula'		d	4-6m	(12-18ft)
Sorbus aucuparia 'Pendula'	Rowan	d	5m	(15ft)
Syringa pekinensis 'Pendula'	Lilac	d	3-5m	(10-15ft)
Tamarix juniperina	Tamarisk	d	3-5m	(10-15ft)
Taxus baccata 'Dovastonii'	Yew	e	7-10m	(20-30ft)
Tilia petiolaris	Lime	d	20m	(60ft)
Tsuga canadensis pendula	Hemlock	e	3-5m	(10-15ft)

The fastigiate and severely upright trees are less numerous than the weeping but make a longer list than one would imagine whilst touring round gardens. There are few things as lovely as a mature beech tree but even a youngster in most gardens will quickly outgrow its site. *Fagus sylvatica* 'Dawyck' makes a slender column that will be fine in most gardens for several years. 'Dawyck Purple' allows us to enjoy some of the splendid strength of beech trees as well as the theatrical dark dress of the mahogany foliage.

The Fastigiate and Columnar
(Heights given are for maturity, many will achieve only half or two-thirds in the planter's lifetime.)

Calocedrus decurrens (formerly *Libocedrus)* is the incense cedar capable of 50-75m (60-90ft)

		deciduous/ evergreen	ultimate height	
Abies alba pyramidalis	Silver Fir	e	10m	(30ft)
Acer lobelii	Maple	d	10-15m	(30-45ft)
saccharinum 'Pyramidale'	Sugar Maple	d	12m	(30-40ft)
Aesculus hippocastanum 'Pyramidalis'	Horse Chestnut	d	10-17m	(30-50ft)
Aralia elata 'Pyramidalis'	Angelica Tree	d	7-10m	(20-30ft)
Betula pendula 'Fastigiata'	Birch	d	15-20m	(45-60ft)
Carpinus betulus 'Columnaris'	Hornbeam	d	16m	(50ft)
b. 'Pyramidalis'		d	16m	(50ft)
Castanea sativa 'Pyramidalis'	Sweet Chestnut	d	25m	(80ft)
Cephalotaxus pedunculata 'Fastigiata'		e	3m	(10ft)
Chamaecyparis lawsoniana 'Columnaris'		3	12-15m	(40-50ft)
l.erecta viridis		e	12-15m	(40-50ft)
sempervirens 'Fastigiata'		e	20m	(60ft)
Crataegus monogyna 'Stricta'	Hawthorn	d	3-6m	(15-25ft)
Fagus sylvatica 'Dawyck' 'Dawyck Gold' 'Dawyck Purple'	Beech	d	20m	(60ft)
Juniperus chinensis 'Monarch'	Juniper	e	3-7m	(10-20ft)
communis 'Fastigiata'		e	3-7m	(10-20ft)
Liriodendron tulipifera 'Fastigiatum'	Tulip Tree	d	8-15m	(25-45ft)
Morus alba 'Fastigiata'	Mulberry	d	7-10m	(20-30ft)
Picea abies 'Stricta'	Spruce	e	20m	(60ft)
Pinus sylvestris 'Fastigiata'	Pine	e	20m	(60ft)
Populus alba 'Pyramidalis'	Poplar	d	17-23m	(50-70ft)
nigra 'Italica'	Lombardy Poplar	d	13-23m	(40-70ft)
n. 'Therestina'		d	13-23m	(40-70ft)
simonii 'Fastigiata'		d	7-10m	(20-30ft)
Prunus x hillieri 'Spire'	Cherry	d	3-5m	(10-15ft)
padus 'Stricta'	Bird Cherry	d	10m	(30ft)
P. 'Amanogawa'	Cherry	d	6m	(20ft)
simonii		d	5-7m	(15-20ft)
Ptelea trifoliata 'Fastigiata'		d	7m	(20ft)
Quercus pedunculata 'Fastigiata'	Oak	d	13-20m	(40-60ft)
Robinia pseudoacacia 'Fastigiata'		d	13-20m	(40-60ft)
p. 'Monophylla Fastigiata'		d	13-20m	(40-60ft)
Taxus baccata 'Fastigiata'	Irish Yew	e	7-8m	(20-25ft)
Thuja plicata 'Pyramidalis'	Red Cedar	e	18m	(55ft)

Mass and Form
Most architectural of trees are the evergreens led by the conifers. They are the heavyweights; their solid masses lend a sense of perma-

Glorious early-autumn colour of the weeping beech, *Fagus sylvatica* 'Pendula'

nence. Deciduous trees take on new leaves, bloom, develop mature summer foliar cover, and then turn colour in autumn before being left as silhouettes against grey wintry skies.

Of course, the deciduous have mass. Silver birches are light and feminine, but oaks and beeches have considerable trunks and branches to add to the weight of their leafy cover. The darker these leaves, the heavier the effect.

The extremes of gymnastic posture, the weeping and the fastigiate, are acknowledged, but other forms can be almost as important. The geometrical *Zelkova carpinifolia* remind one of the wooden cut-out trees that come with a Noah's Ark set. No twiglet is out of place in the tightly packed, somewhat upwardly but widely inclined straight branches. Here is a tree for the obsessively tidy gardener.

Some whitebeams are not too far behind the *Zelkova* in forming basic tree-shaped trees. *Sorbus aria* is variable but I think it probably has no poor forms. Most immediately decorative is *S.a.* 'Majestica' with leaves maybe over 15cm (6in) long and as much as 10cm (4in) wide. Its first act of the year is to allow the opening buds to unwrap brilliantly silver-white infant leaves and hold them like so many candles set along the wide dark branches. It makes many a flowering tree look dowdy. Leaves unfurl fully but retain the bright white felt underneath. Upper surfaces, slightly silken-haired in youth, become polished dark green. But in May, while the leaves are still young, the many 10cm (4in) wide corymbs of creamy-white flowers produce a second highlighted season. Through the summer the neat correct form of the tree and its handsome foliage continue to attract admiration. Summer's end brings bright orange scarlet fruits with darker speckles, which attract the birds to enjoy the juicy bounty.

There are one-off types easily accommodated. Does the monkey puzzle tree, *Araucaria arucana,* bewilder monkeys? The Hankow corkscrew tree, *Salix matsudana* 'Tortuosa' is almost as curious in shape with erratically curling branches making a useful contribution to the garden scene. The narrow pale-green leaves are typical of willow foliage but these too are twisted.

Acer   maples and sycamores

Few families of shrubs and trees can challenge these for beauty of foliage. Many maples are slow growing and, although capable of forming very elegant small trees eventually, gardeners are best advised to look on them as shrubs (see next chapter). The sycamores and some other acers grow much more quickly to tree status.

A.campestre: common maple   d   5 to 10m (15 to 30ft)
The wild maple of our hedgerows left unmolested makes a lovely tree. The neatly lobed foliage is bright green through the main months; in spring it often unfurls in warm shades of pink and red; in the autumn it becomes a hundred-and-one golds, oranges, and reds. Selected forms are offered by a few growers.

A.cappadocicum 'Rubrum' *(A.colchicum rubrum)*   d   12 to 20m
(40 to 60ft)
Slow to reach its upper limits and so may be thought of as medium
sized. Young leaves are rich reds. Mature five- or seven-pointed
lobed leaves are a lively green.

A.cissifolium   d   7 to 10m (20 to 30ft)
Leaves are divided into three leaflets 5 to 10cm (2 to 4in) long. They
are roughly serrated. Both surfaces are shining green. One of the
better autumn colourers, brilliant in golds and reds. It makes a
rounded, much-branched small tree.

A.davidii   d   10 to 17m (30 to 50ft)
Useful distinct character with undivided leaves that can be impres-
sively large, 15 to 20cm (6 to 8in) long and shiny green. New,
younger bark is pencilled with white stripes. Young leaves are
suffused red; in the autumn they abandon everyday green for gold,
orange and red.

A.ginnala   d   3 to 7m (10 to 20ft)
One of the very best autumn colourists, then resplendent in crimson red. Leaves are a rich green through the year and are clearly
three lobed, measuring overall perhaps 9 by 6cm wide (3½ by
2½in). It may spend quite a few years masquerading effectively as a
shrub before attaining small-tree status.

A.lobelii   d   28m (50ft)
An erect strong tree with palmate five-lobed leaves up to 18cm
(7in) long.

A.negundo: box elder   d   12 to 20m (40 to 60ft)
Usually seen in its variegated forms, *A.n.* 'Aureovariegatum' and *A.n.*
'Variegatum'. These are rarely more than half the heights of the type.
'Variegatum' is most widely planted; the pinnate leaves 12 to 25cm
(5 to 10in) long, having three or five leaflets each up to 10cm (4in)
long, and painted broadly with creamy white along the leaf margins
— often a wavering stroke that can sometimes engulf the whole leaf.
The 'Aureovariegatum' form has gold rather than creamy-white
variegation. These well-formed rounded pyramidal trees light up
the whole area.

A.palmatum: Japanese maple   d   7m (20ft)
This popular species makes a narrow-trunked dainty rounded tree
in time, but will be shrub sized for long enough and so it is listed
under shrubs; one of the most important of all foliar plants.

A.pensylvanicum: snake bark maple   d   5 to 8m (15 to 25ft)
Much valued for its foliage and for the white zigzag striping of the
younger bark, and the neat erect growth. Large leaves, maybe over
15cm (6in) long, are three pointed and after a pink-flushed infancy

become a splendid adult green before eventually turning gold and falling. Young stems of *A.p.* 'Erythrocladum' still give colour, a polished crimson, after leaves have fallen.

A.platanoides: Norway maple   d   20m+ (60ft+)
This tree, of exemplary worth in many ways, is too big and quick growing for the smaller gardens, though some forms are more restricted. 'Crimson King' with polished mahogany-red leaves, boldly five lobed, can be dramatic.

A.pseudoplatanus: sycamore   d   35m (100ft)
Too big and brash for the garden. The form 'Brilliantissimum' is smaller and much slower growing. It distinguishes itself with gorgeous young foliage in coral pinks. These glowing shades become more golden and then lemony before donning orthodox green.

A.rubrum: red maple   d   16 to 20m (50 to 60ft)
Eventually too large for normal gardens, but slow growing. Palmate leaves turn gold and red in autumn. Through the summer they are dark green above and blue-white below.

A.rufinerve   d   7 to 10m (20 to 30ft)
Altogether pleasing. Lobed leaves are a rich green above and pale below. When newly unfurled the stalks and leaves are usually red. The autumn colours can end a very deep crimson. Leaves are three

Acer glade at Westonbirt
Arboretum *(Author)*

lobed, in youth the lower surfaces have a certain amount of reddish-brown felty fluff gathered along the veins.

A.saccharinum: sugar maple   d   25m (80ft)
Too quick to attain giant forest-tree dimensions. The form 'Elegant' is still large but rather more circumspect in manner and compact form. 'Pyramidale' is erect growing, almost fastigiate.

Aesculus x carnea: red horse chestnut   d   1 to 17m (30 to 50ft)
A considerable rounded tree, smaller and darker in leaf than the common horse chestnut. Grows quickly to 3 to 7m (15 to 20ft). Typical candelabras of flowers 15 to 24cm (6 to 9in) high and a rich dark red. Healthy short-stalked leaves in five or seven leaflets making together a dark mass, dying off golden yellow and brown. *A.c.* 'Briottii' is a more useful selection as it is more compact in form and is even more richly coloured in bloom.

Ailanthus altissima (glandulosa): tree of heaven   d   16 to 28m
                                                                          (50 to 80ft)
Reaching upwards to justify its common name. Obviously too large for most, but its pinnate foliage is very attractive on young saplings. These leaves are often 1m (3ft) long composed of over a dozen to maybe more than 30 leaflets 15 to 25cm (6 to 10in) long. Mature specimens spend energy more discreetly with leaves of half the size. The foliage is always attractive.
    This reacts to strict discipline by maximising leaf size. Young plants are cut down virtually to soil level. One stem only is allowed from the resulting growth. This will bear leaves as long as 1 to 1.4m (3 to 4ft) of many clean-cut leaflets all held in a proud horizontal manner.

Alnus: the alders
Proletarian trees not without attraction against water, but for the countryside rather than for the garden.

A.cordata: Italian alder   d   16m to 28m (50 to 80ft)
Altogether a snappier dresser than our wild alder with larger, more rounded, heart-shaped polished leaves. A fine pyramidal tree in moist or wet ground. Grows quickly. Could prove too large unless pollarded or removed before reaching maturity.

Aralia elata: angelica tree   d   7 to 10m (20 to 30ft)
Expensive young shrubs grow steadily to make sparingly branched small trees. At all stages it is one of the finest of foliage plants. Huge pinnate, or rather doubly pinnate, leaves can often measure 90cm to 1.2m (3 to 4ft). These massive cleanly tailored leaves cut glorious patterns in the airspace giving an impression of opulent size that is severely shaken when we regard the bare branches after leaf fall. The wide-reaching pose of the leaves displays them to their very best advantage.

The type is plain green but variegated forms grab the limelight. Many gardeners would place the gold- and the white-margined kinds as joint winners of the award for 'the best variegated plant.' *A.e.* 'Variegata' has each pointed oval leaflet boldly but unevenly margined milk white, the green of the main leaf blade being toned down with a pale filter. *A.e.* 'Aureovariegata' is similar but with golden colouring that is just as strikingly painted, perhaps over half of each leaf blade being coloured. To build up a strong-trunked specimen it should be grown in a reasonable well-drained soil but not one that is overly rich. The wood looks soft and it should not be weakened by forced feeding. Greeny-white flowers are tiny individually but, as they are produced in large numbers in a complex panicle that can be 30 to 60 cm (1 to 2ft) long and almost as much wide, it is a most effective sight in late summer.

Arbutus

These belong to the heather family. The one native to southern Ireland is *A.unedo.* Two other species are sometimes grown, *A.andrachne* and *A.menziesii. A.x andrachnoides* is the hybrid race between *A.andrachne* and *A.unedo;* the hybrids are probably commonest but none is seen as widely as they deserve. All are handsome, tough-leaved evergreens building up cloud-shaped shrubs that later become trees. Flowers are typical of the heathers.

A.unedo: strawberry tree   e   5 to 8m (15 to 25ft)

Polished leaves of dark green are 5 to 10cm (2 to 4in) long and 1 to 4cms (1 to 1½in) wide. Rich heavy masses of foliage can be enjoyed in most gardens because this is one of very few ericaceous plants uninhibited by lime. It has 5cm (2in) long white or blush-pink sprays of flowers and the tough, orange 2cm (¾in) tough-skinned strawberry-like fruits. Hanging flower sprays are displayed from autumn through to Christmas at the same time as the fruits are ripening from last year's blossom, a focus of interest during the duller part of the gardening year.

A.andrachne   e   5 to 8m (15 to 25ft)

This rarity has evergreen leaves at least as long as those typical of *A.unedo* but broader. Newer stems are smooth, those of *A.unedo* are hairy. White flowers arrive in spring.

A.x andrachnoides   e   5 to 8m (15 to 25ft)

The hybrid progeny of the previous two species vary according to the extent they favour one or other parent, but are all somewhat more vigorous and are worth growing. Main flushes of white bloom occur in autumn and spring, and these are likely to be bigger than those of either parent whilst the gently serrated foliage is rich, polished, and first-class material all the year round.

Betula: birches

The birches have light leaves in keeping with their total graceful aura; the foliage is pleasing but may play a supporting role to the silver bark of some and the overall character of most. Useful in medium-sized gardens, they fairly quickly reach a size to make a significant contribution and are pleasing in and out of leaf. Fresh green colour can become a glowing uniform chrome yellow before falling quite early in the autumn.

B.ermanii   d   17m (50ft)
Trunks are buffy white and peel to reveal rich shades of brown and chrome. Autumn leaves are bright gold.

B.jacquemontii   d   15+m (45+ft)
Star of the genus with vividly white peeling bark, this white extending close to the slender new stems. The habit of the tree is upright with plenty of branches forming a pyramidal shape. It can upstage many fine things but is at its most daring in the limelight that bathes it through the winter. Typical birch foliage is firmer and larger than most silver birches.

B. pendula (verrucosa): silver birch   d   10 to 14m (30 to 40ft)
One of the silver birches of our countryside, the lesser branches arch downwards to add grace to the whole ensemble. Foliage is lighter than that of *B.jacquemontii.*

Carpinus betulus: hornbeam   d   16m+ (50ft+)
The beeches are magnificent; many would argue that the hornbeams are equally splendid but more balanced, graceful trees. Mature specimens make wonderful rounded pyramid designs with good trunks and with plenty of low branches reaching near soil level. Leaves are narrower than those of the beeches and are clearly serrated. Far too big to grow as a garden specimen, it is featured here because of its great value as a hedging plant and by virtue of one or two varieties that are less spreading.

Of deciduous contenders for 'best hedging plant' the hornbeam could win. With common or the fastigiate form, one can make an intricate neat hedge of almost any conceivable height furnished with healthy green from tip to toe. Leaves are rougher than those of beech, but through the winter till the spring the rusty-brown dead-leaf cover is more sure and persistent than that of beeches.

C.b. 'Fastigiata' is a conspicuous steeple of a tree; 'Pyramidalis' grows uprightly but less constrainedly tight.

Catalpa bignonioides: Indian bean tree   d   7 to 14m (20 to 40ft)
Makes a fine specimen tree with outstanding leaves and sensible form. A firm trunk supports relatively few branches that on mature individuals will allow lesser branches to hang downwards close to the ground so that we may admire its wares. Simple broad ovate leaves are large, the smallest perhaps 10cm (4in) long and almost as wide, but with most much larger and some close to 30cm (1ft) long

and 25cm (10in) wide. Such opulence suggests the exotic, but its effect is achieved with a simple decorum only becoming dramatic when in bloom, having broad panicles of many white flowers with yellow and purple spots. The foliage dies off yellow (see page 37).

After two and a half centuries we persist in calling this the Indian bean tree but it is the American Indians who are so remembered; this species comes from Eastern North America. With only room for one it may be best to plant 'Aurea' with equally huge highlighted leaves; young leaves are light yellow staying bright even if a little greener in the summer months. They turn deeper yellow and gold before dropping.

Cedrus

The cedars become huge trees. Tempting baby ones are to be found in neat rows in garden centres; they will need felling long, long before maturity. Some forms need less space, and because young plants provide good evergreen foliage they are listed.

C.atlantica: Atlas cedar   e   35m (100ft)

Dark-green tree, a pyramid in youth but in later years a massive horizontally branched kind like the Cedar of Lebanon. 'Glauca', with silver-blue foliage, makes a spectacular specimen tree, needing space to do itself justice, a wide lawn rather than cramped in a small plot. For anyone with a penchant for the curious the weeping form, 'Glauca Pendula', is interesting. An upright trunk is designed like a

Cercidiphyllum japonicum with wide spreading branches of heart-shaped leaves; bright healthy green in full growth and dying off to rich golds, oranges, and reds. Seen here at Winkworth Arboretum

slender metal pole. A few branches fall vertically and are whipped close into the trunk. The top, where the leading growth continues ever onward, may be looped over, as curved as an umbrella handle. It takes up almost as much space as a small telegraph pole (and the aesthetic appeal is about as great in some people's estimation).

C.deodara: deodar   e   35m ((100ft)
Another giant but lovely in its youth, making a tall conical shape of more or less pendulous branches well clothed with 3 to 5cm (1 to 2in) long grey-green needles.

C.libani: Cedar of Lebanon   e   35m (100ft)
Huge; green, somewhat grey-green, in leaf; pyramidal in form before becoming mature.

Cercidiphyllum japonicum   d   2 to 7m (8 to 20ft)
Usually a shrub in this country but over 35m (100ft) high in the East. Whatever its stature there is no doubting the brilliance of its autumn colouring. Broadly ovate flat leaves, 5 to 10cm (2 to 4in) long and almost as wide, become shades of vivid gold, orange, and red in autumn.

Cercis siliquastrum: Judas tree   d   4 to 10m (12 to 30ft)
Best of the genus in Britain but having some difficulty deciding whether to be a shrub or a real tree. Foliage is rounded, and unusual in being somewhat broader than long. Leaves may be 10cm (4in) across and a good green with glaucous grey overtone. Clusters of pea flowers shining purplish pink decorate it overall in late spring. The succeeding flat peapods are suffused purple; they lose their colour in the autumn and winter but still hang from the bare branches.

Chamaecyparis
Of the species gathered in this family the most important is *C.law-soniana* in all its manifestations. *C.nootkatensis* is a fine tall robust species but is likely to outgrow its space and welcome rapidly. *C.obtusa* and *C.pisifera* are inclined to be more open in growth, especially as they age. These are more robust than the true Cupressuses.

C.lawsoniana: Lawson cypress   e   35m (100ft)
Whilst most varieties can grow high and rapidly in youth, they are always attractive. Having reached some 5 to 7m (15 to 20ft) they steady their rate of advance. Visit a good collection before deciding on your choice. Among the many likely contenders for your garden space are these:
'Allumii'; a popular blue-green type of dense columnar form.
'Columnariis'; sometimes listed as 'Columnaris Glauca'; narrow column of blue-green foliage.
'Ellwoodii'; slow growing, tightly formed, grey-green often offered

Chamaecyparis lawsoniana 'Wissellii' is one of a long series of forms of this variable, most useful species

as a dwarf but slowly, slowly outgrowing this classification.
'Ellwood's Gold'; a similar slow, upright darkish-green kind with younger foliage yellowish especially in spring.
'Golden Spire'; upright form with golden foliage becoming bronzed, even orange, in winter.
'Pembury Blue'; very striking with narrow dense elongated pyramid of very blue foliage glistening in the sunlight.
'Spek' ('Glauca Spek'); bright blue-green form.
'Triumph of Boskoop'; old clone of broadly conical form with dark leaves tipped blue-grey.

C.nootkatensis 'Pendula'; very dramatic kind with branches curving down and outwards. Branches are bare above but hung below with long tresses of rich-green foliage.

Cupressocyparis leylandii: Leyland cypress   e   35m (100ft)
The hybrid between *Cypressus macrocarpa* and *Chamaecyparis nootkatensis.* Makes very tall columns of dark green, but more than ninety-nine out of every hundred are used for hedges. 'Castlewellan Gold' is a bright golden form that makes an attractive specimen tree as well as a cheerful hedge.

Cladrastis tinctoria (lutea): yellow woad   d   10m (30ft)
Member of the pea family eventually making a rounded wide tree grown for its foliage. Leaves up to 30cm (1ft) long are pinnate with a normal count of seven or nine oval leaflets. The shining green of the growing months advertises health, in the autumn all is transmuted to gold. It is not a free bloomer, but when it does bunches of typical pea-white flowers hang from the branch ends.

Clerodendron trichotomum   d   3 to 5m (10 to 15ft)
A shrubby small tree. Ovate leaves can be impressive sizes on young energetic plants — may be 22 x 12cm (9 x 5in). The angular up-ward habit of the plant is not its best feature. The foliage is pleasing enough, the flowering effort in white is considerable, but this is followed by crowded bunches of fruits lasting after leaf-fall until well beyond Christmas. It is grown for this off-season performance. Many clusters of shining round little beads are a most unusual violet blue. *C.t.fargesii* is freer fruiting and more resistant to frost.

Cornus florida: flowering dogwood   d   3 to 7m (10 to 20ft)
A classic shrub, and in the fullness of time, a small tree that does best without late spring frosts. Foliage is of broad oval leaves but pointed, and a rich deep green. Autumn colour can be brilliantly scarlet red and crimson. 'Flowers', really four bracts, are formed in the autumn and unfurl white in late spring.

C.kousa   d   3 to 7m (10 to 20ft)
Be it a shrub or small tree, this is a fine character. Foliage of oval-pointed leaves up to 7cm (3in) long and half as wide makes a

healthy green background for the upright flowers on the more or
less horizontal branches. The four bracts are larger and more
pointed than those of *C.florida.* Starting greenish they become
white in due season, before browning with age. *C.k.chinensis* has
large creamy flowers, whilst 'China Girl' is perhaps the largest
flowering selection yet. All have sumptuous crimson-red autumn
colours.

Corylus colurna: Turkish hazel   d   17m (50ft)
Unusual amongst hazels in forming a tree, and a very substantial one
at that. Its foliage, 7 to 15cm (3 to 6in) long is hazel-like. It has the
usual appendages, catkins and nuts. The leaf cover is pleasing, the
bark is corky.

Crataegus: thorns
Of hundreds of ornamental thorns, many make fine specimens of
not too large stature, and full of character. While not first-rank
foliage plants, one or two are rather ahead of the ruck in this respect.
The Glastonbury thorn, *C.monogyna* 'Praecox', produces flurries of
flower in winter, maybe at Christmas and maybe not, and comes
into leaf early. *C.x grignonensis* is a strong growing thornless thorn.
Leathery strong leaves are present and correct, probably until the
end of the year. Blossom is followed by brownish-red haws that may
well hang on until spring. *C.x lavellei (C.x carrierei)* makes a tough
tree 3 to 6m (15 to 20ft) high. Polished dark-green leaves last into
winter, whilst orange-red fruits can persist till spring.

Davidia involucrata: handkerchief tree   d   8 to 15m (20 to 45ft)
Slow growing, perfectly hardy Chinese tree with good rounded
leaves some 7 to 15cm (3 to 6in) long and nearly as wide. It has a
sturdy trunk and well-spaced, upward-reaching main branches with
lesser ones arching. Leaves may or may not be conspicuously white
on their under surfaces. The large white bracts hang out as 'handker-
chiefs' for weeks in the summer.

Eucalyptus
Few of the 600 species wild in Australia will find Britain an acceptable substitute, but the few are likely to be more than the one or two
at present widely grown. *E.gunnii* is the favourite because of its
hardiness and the attractiveness of the juvenile foliage.
E.niphophila is even hardier with lovely bark and fine metallic
leaves. From the high ground of Tasmania there may be several
species that will prove hardy, some strains or clones of species may
be hardier than others. Eucalyptus are rapid growers and particularly useful in new gardens. They contribute a distinctive new
design element.

E.gunnii: cider gum   e   7 to 15m (20 to 40ft)
From seed, nurserymen can have saleable plants a metre — three or
four feet — high within one growing season. These look good with

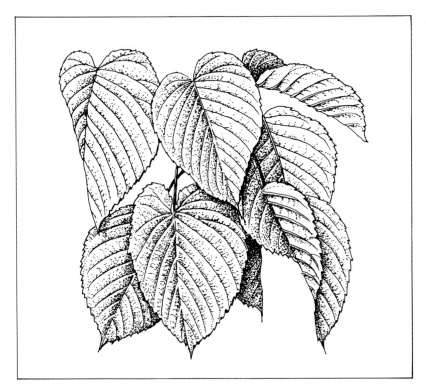

Davidia involucrata is a handsome foliage tree whose large white bracts give it its common name handkerchief tree. Later it has large round fruits dangling on very long stems

upright stems well clothed with round leaves closely held. One choice for the gardener is to allow the plant to grow upright, quickly making a considerable tree with graceful branches holding adult flat, spear-shaped pointed leaves. They sparkle in grey-green metallic shades. Alternatively the plant can be established but then be cut down almost to the ground. Resulting new growth returns to the lovely silvery round leaves of youth, a fountain of flashing colour. This cutting back can be repeated frequently, perhaps every two years. The ideal may be to have a couple of specimens, alternating the coppicing each April.

E.niphophila: alpine snow gum   e   7 to 15m (20 to 40ft)
Amongst those we have raised of this fine species there is variation both in the colouring of the bark and the branch formation. Trees are always pleasing. Younger bark is often a beautiful silver; this peels away to reveal olive, fawn, or pinky colours. Young leaves and stems can be a shining pinky-orange red, the tough flat spear-shaped mature leaves point downwards and are grouped in dense bunches towards the branch ends. Individual leaves measure up to 13cm (5in) long and 3 to 4cm (1½in) wide.

E.cordata   e   14m (40ft)
This is worth trying even if it never reaches the mature size and height possible in favoured places like Cornwall. Seedlings can be used for summer bedding. In their second year they will be more

than head high. Foliage is rounded and much larger than that of *E.gunnii*. These discs are held tight to the stem without stalks and measure to 2 to 8cm (1 to 3in) long and almost as wide. Colour is vivid silver white over a blue-grey base, one of the brightest of all. This colour and the astonishing strength of the seedlings make it a focus of attention; against a dark background of holly, or yew, the eucalypt will be powerfully spotlighted. Winter colour is rather more an amalgam of grey-blue and green but still with a metallic gleam.

E.nicholii   e   10m (30ft)
The height is a guess as I can find no full description of this species. We hope that will prove hardy. It is quite distinct. Our specimens have very thin silver-grey strips as leaves, each not wider than about 3mm (¹⁄₁₀in) but perhaps 5cm (2in) long. Young stems and foliage are pinky-orange, stems are thread thin. Midribs of leaves are often orange flushed. The whole is light and airy. Even if coppiced, they will be treasured plants.

Eucryphia glutinosa   d/e   3 to 7m (10 to 20ft)
With us, this is usually an evergreen with polished, very dark-green leaves. The shrub and then tree is of upward stance. It is a lime hater and once established, preferably not in the full glare of the sun, it shoots up quickly. Foliage cover is very dark and polished, a contrast to the white midsummer flowers that are four petalled with a golden centre of stamens.

Grey-green *E.nicholii* (below) is enlivened with pinky-red stems and veins. *E.cordata* has large leaves flashing silver white. *E.gunnii* (top and right) with round young leaves and spear-shaped older ones is silver grey, its popularity being challenged by a number of more recently introduced kinds

Fagus sylvatica: beech
Beeches are too large for normal gardens, although used for hedging and there are fastigiate ones. Hedges, usually of the type, may have one in ten copper coloured to add interest. Random distribution of the copper ones is most pleasing. Young foliage is of appealing fresh-ness, soft and silky to the touch and vividly green. Adult foliage is tough, darker, and rich. Tight clipping retains much orangey-brown dead leaves through the first half of the winter, useful warm colour in bleak times. *F.s.*'Dawyck' *(fastigiata)* makes a tight column of branches clothed with typical green beech leaves. There is a newer purple-leaved equivalent, 'Dawyck Purple', which is very dramatic. Contrast in form and colour between this and something like the golden-leaved Indian bean tree, *Catalpa bignonioides* 'Aurea', can be good garden theatre.

Ginkgo biloba: maidenhair tree   d   7 to 15m (20 to 40ft)
This interesting 'fossil' tree looks different. It makes an upright rather than a spreading tree, upward pointing branches having plastic fan-shaped leaves of light green that turn gold before dropping. Unique leaf form.

Gleditsia triacanthos: honey locust   d   20m (60ft)
The honey locust has no pretensions about floral beauty, small greenish working parts. It is grown for divided, ferny foliage in rich shining greens. Leaves are 10 to 22cm (4 to 9in) long, the usual ones being pinnate, but stronger ones being doubly pinnate. Each leaf may have up to 30 leaflets so giving rise to the ferny effect. Autumn colour is gold.

Gymnocladus dioicus (canadensis): Kentucky coffee tree   d   20m (60ft)
Has wonderful, huge, beautiful leaves. Trees are slow growing, not reaching half the ultimate measure in a gardener's lifetime. With ini-tially a few main thick branches, it stands in the winter like some posing Mr Muscleman of the arborial world. At any age its pinnate leaves are great, maybe 1m (3ft) long and over 60cm (2ft) wide. Starting from the lowest divisions of the leaf, there are a couple of opposite straightforward ovate leaflets. Upper divisions will be sub-divided again into four to seven further leaflets. There may be one to five pairs of these divisions. The lowest simple leaflets can be as much as 12cm (5in) long, but the bipinnate leaflets can be 2 to 7cm (1 to 3in).
    Summer dress is grey-green, but young leaves emerge in lovely soft-pink shades and in autumn the green is filtered away to leave all a clear yellow. Leaflets fall in succession in autumn but the main stalks are left pointing all around, hedgehog-wise, till these too fall and the bare sturdy body is left.

Halesia carolina: snowdrop tree   d   7 to 8m (20 to 25ft)
Judged by foliage this is no mean shrub or tree, but its main claim to

fame is its flowers. In late spring the spreading branches are alive with unfurling leaves and along the length of the previous year's wood are hung lots of little white bells. It is stylish and charming. Bells are 1 to 1.5cm (½ to ¾in) long and hung in bunches of up to half a dozen. Leaves grow on, pointed ovals and 5 to 15cm (2 to 6in) long. Below they are furry grey, above they are green, made slightly greyish by far fewer hairs.

Ilex: the hollies

The lacquered good health and hardiness makes for great year-round value. They could look too funereally dark were it not for the polished laminated surfaces. Hard edged, spiny margins and surface undulations ensure light playing on them to give added liveliness. The common holly makes an impressive tree eventually, but the young shrubby state of this and all the other variants is just as pleasing. If planted in reasonable soil they may seem slow for their first and second years but will then begin to make a steady rate of expansion.

Many kinds are offered. They are best seen before buying, some being rather lax in growth and others, interesting to read about, are

The beech *Fagus sylvatica* 'Cockleshell' at the Hillier Arboretum

not to my mind worth their space. The hedgehog holly *I.aquifolium* 'Ferox', sounds interesting (we all like hedgehogs) but is best left to collectors of curiosities because of its pimply foliage. Leaf surfaces erupt in a rash of pimples and prickles especially towards the ends and sides.

A short list of good forms is offered. The multiplicity of variegated types underlines their importance; I feel those with colour confined to the margins are wholly more decorative than those with the centre coloured. Holly nomenclature is a minefield; purchase by appearance rather than by relying on the seller's labelling. If you want berries you must have plants of both sexes, one male will serve several females. Just to confuse the unwary, common names are no guide to gender, 'Silver Queen' and 'Golden Queen' are males, whilst 'Golden King' is a prolific female. All very contrary!

I.x altaclarensis 'Belgica'; grows tall with impressive large dark leaves and fat orange-red fruits.

'Golden King'; this is a fine golden variegated form less thornily armed than most and with good red berries.

I.aquifolium 'Bacciflava'; a tall columnar tree with rather pendulous branches. Fine dark foliage and yellow berries.

'Golden Van Tol'; a bright golden variegated one with no spines.

The hollies *Ilex* 'Golden King' (right) and *I.x. altaclerenis* 'Lawsoniana'. Below *I.a.* 'Ferox' and *I.crenata*

'Handsworth Silver'; an excellent kind, silver margined spiny leaves with good crops of berries.

'J.C. Van Tol'; good straightforward dark holly with plenty of orange-red berries.

'Mme Briot'; a well-berried, spiny, kind with the golden variegation irregularly marking the leaves, sometimes just the margins, sometimes moving to the centre, and on occasions turning whole leaves or sprays of leaves yellow.

Juglans nigra: black walnut   d   26m (80ft)
This is an altogether more dashing character than our native tree which is itself no mean performer. The black walnut grows quicker and has very handsome leaves from 30 to 60cm (1 to 2ft) long and made up of polished full-green leaflets. There is usually an end leaflet, but not always, so that a leaf may have from 10 to 11 to 22 to 23, each leaflet being 5 to 15cm (2 to 6in) long. Its clean, dark trunk supports the framework of well-spaced branches of a well-designed pyramidal tree, particularly impressive as a young specimen. True, it makes a massive tree and cannot be everyone's choice, but in youth it is all splendid healthy extrovert growth.

Juniperus
The junipers are a very variable lot. Where the common juniper, *J.communis,* grows in Britain this variability can be quickly appreciated; some look little more than spreading shrubs though they are manifestly old plants. Others may grow more restrainedly upright and make reasonable trees. They can vary from less than 3m (9ft) to 10m (30ft). What gardeners are offered are the propagated clones of selected good individuals.

J.chinensis: the Chinese juniper and *J.virginiana* are the best garden tree species. *J.c.* 'Blue Point' is a conical evergreen of tight blue-shaded leaves. *J.c.* 'Keteleerii' is one of the tallest growing clones, a good pyramid of rich green. 'Monarch' is one of the narrow architectural cone or column kinds in grey-blue.

J.communis 'Hibernica' (fastigiata):   the Irish juniper makes a perfect narrow upright column perhaps 3 to 7m (10 to 20ft) tall but only 60cm to 1m (2 to 3ft) through.

J.virginiana: pencil cedar   Many clones have been named and introduced, some dwarf and spreading, but the tree forms can grow to become the tallest of the genus in Britain. 'Glauca' is long established, of pyramid mass and most silvery blue in the growing months of spring and summer, somewhat greener later. At present the most popular form is 'Skyrocket', a good name for such a slender upright plant that shoots up quickly to make a tall, very tidy narrow column.

Koelreutera paniculata: golden rain tree   d   10m (30ft)
Planted in a warm sunny site, a seedling tree grows fast to form a
sparse upright sapling that will fill out in a later years. Splendid pinnate or bipinnate leaves usually have around a dozen leaflets. Each
of these leaflets measure up to 10cm (4in) but the whole leaf can be
about 60cm (2ft) long, though this is exceptional. Leaflets have
well-marked veining and serrated margins. In midsummer many tall
cone-shaped panicles are held upright and there is a mass of rich
golden small flowers. Leaves become golden before falling.

Larix decidua: European larch   d   30m (90ft)
There is no more pleasing larch than the common one, perhaps no
foliage is a fresher green than its new young growth.

Laurus nobilis: bay laurel, sweet bay   e   13m (40ft)
One of the oldest introduced trees and capable of forming intricately branched masses of dark bay leaves. Lots of upright stems
support a pyramidal form. Often pruned into topiary shapes.

Liquidamber styraciflua: sweet gum   d   20m (60ft)
This makes an elegant, upright tree with attractive maple-like
foliage. Five- or seven-lobed leaves are up to 18cm (7in) wide,
16cms (6½in) in length. Glossy green gives way to very rich brilliant reds and oranges in the autumn, one of the best performers at
this season.

Liriodendron tulipifera: tulip tree   d   35m (100ft)
Magnificent, tall, stately tree for large gardens or parks. Foliage is impressive for size and unusual shape, distinctly wider than long and
the length will be in the 8 to 22cm (3 to 9in) range. Leaf tops appear
to be clipped off. Healthy polished light green turns to clear golds in
the autumn. Foliage can be enjoyed in the closely fastigiate form,
'Fastigiatum', the unusual, large tulip flowers in light greens and pale
orange start appearing fairly early in its life.

Magnolias

Whilst glorious in blossom, they are a touch ordinary in leaf. An exception is the evergreen *M. grandiflora.* In the open the best specimens are to be seen wherever the Gulf Stream is working efficiently,
elsewhere it grows well with the warmth of a wall. Here, it is best
securely tied to the wall so that sudden heavy snowfalls do not
threaten its stability. The neatly arranged foliage cover is of strong,
highly polished laurel-like leaves. These are often over 15cm (6in)
long and, in some cases, close to twice this length. Under-surfaces
have a gingery, chocolate felt which is a decorative contrast; this
tends to lose some of its nap with age. Most important variant is
M. g. lanceolata (exoniensis), the Exmouth magnolia. Leaves are
distinctly narrower but the vital difference is its greater hardiness
and its welcome habit of blooming as a youngster, much earlier than
the type.

Large leaves of the tulip tree
Liriodendrum tulipifera, with
unusually formed leaves and
unique flowers

Malus

Apples can make character trees, often dark trunked and spellbinding in bloom, with brilliantly coloured, unusual shades of foliage. One of the oldest hybrid crabapples is 'Eleyi', dark trunked and dark stemmed; the leaves are also dark, a purplish-red but much brighter in their unfurling youth while the fruits are long-stemmed and rich, dark-purple red. 'Liset' is even darker, glossy purple in leaf, purple fruited. 'Profusion' is another in this mould, wreathed in crimson-red flowers and purple in leaf and fruit.

'Cheal's Weeping' and 'Red Jade' are small trees of distinctly weeping form. 'Red Jade' is a pattern of white and pink in blossom with green leaves. 'Cheal's Weeping' has the foliage suffused purple and flowers a mix of bright lilac tinted red.

Morus: mulberry

M.nigra: common mulberry   d   6 to 10m (20 to 30ft)

The common mulberry makes a fine craggy specimen with a very good cover of ovate leaves well netted with veins and rough to the touch with short bristly hairs. These leaves can be quite a size, up to a maximum 25cm (10in) long. It is not a fast grower. Branches tend to reach downwards, the whole assemblage making an interesting rounded informal shape.

M.alba: white mulberry   d   10 to 15m (30 to 50ft)

Perhaps we could start a silkworm industry in this country by planting a few of this upright, less individualistic mulberry. Leaves are less rough than the common mulberry. The pendulous form *M.a.pendula* is an exception to this mild criticism of the lack of the common mulberry's craggy character. Rounded heads have some branches cascading vertically down. The leading growth needs tying to a well-fixed pole until it is trained up to three metres — fifteen or more feet.

Parrotia persica   d   10m (30ft)

The name sounds exotic. It is from Persia upwards into Russia. In autumn it has all the colours of an eastern bazaar, the leaves, from 5 to 15cm (2 to 6in) long and half as wide, turning from a polished green to a hundred shades of bronze, gold, orange, purple, red and crimson. It can make a fine, tall tree given plenty of time, but if left to its own devices will become a spreading shrub or embryo tree with well-clothed outward and falling branches. This is acceptable, especially where space is limited. On the other hand a little pruning and tethering to a post in youth can provide a trunk tailored to your requirements. Flowers are unspectactular.

Paulownia tomentosa   d   10m (30ft)

This is a fine foliage type and in favoured areas, such as the balmy southwest, it can show what it can be as a floral star. Its habit of producing well-advanced flower buds in the autumn, almost guarantees that the worst happens. The long regime of freezing and unfreezing renders the flower buds useless the following May. The foliage on the other hand is good at all times. Leaves vary much in size; little ones are a simple ovate shape but, when they reach over 12cm (5in) towards a maximum length and width of nearly 30cm (1ft), they acquire three or five sharp-ended but shallowly cut lobes. Rich, dark green above contrasts with woolly grey below.

Playing games with this plant will conjure up five-sided leaves as wide as umbrellas, 60cm to 1m (2 to 3ft) across! These are the rules: plant a young specimen in rich deep soil, get it well established, and then cut it back in the winter to within a finger's length of the soil surface. Allow only two buds to develop then, as spring growth gets underway, reduce all endeavour to a single stem. Feed and water well. Stand back and watch your beanstalk go up to 3m (9ft) or more with leaves of quite eye-boggling sizes. A group of three or five creates an extraordinary sight.

Photinia villosa d 4 to 5m (12 to 15ft)
The genus is related to the thorns and rowans. This species makes a small tree with similar bunches of white flowers followed in the autumn by sizeable, bright red haws. Then the tree comes into its own with wonderful colours. The cultivar *P.v.laevis* is the most commonly offered plant with longish neatly serrated leaves 5 to 12cm (2 to 5in) long and taking fire with vivid oranges and reds before dying away.

Prunus
The cherries have good healthy, if not spectacular, leaves. Buds and infantile leaves may be orange red and after spending a working life in green they change into party dresses of all shades of yellow, orange and red before quickly falling. The smaller-leaved kinds like *P.subhirtella* colour in the same manner, but the autumn season is a fleeting one. *P.sargentii* merits special mention as one of the best dressed of the family and lovely in bloom. It covers itself with a mass of rich pink single flowers in April usually before the young foliage has lost its initial bronze and red pigmentation. Then in autumn it is probably the brightest of the whole family.

Ptelea trifoliata: hop tree d 7m (20ft)
A thickset, statuesque tree with its arms spread wider than high. There are three almost oblong leaflets on each leaf, the biggest, the leading one measures from 6 to 15cm (2½ to 6in), whilst the two supporting leaflets are lop-sided, being better endowed the far side of the midvein. Greenish ivory bunches of flowers are followed by flat fruits akin to those of hops or elms. These are interesting but extremely untidy in the autumn and early winter. What one gardener finds interesting another finds irritating.

Pyrus salicifolia: willow-leaved pear d 5 to 7m (15 to 20ft)
This sensible-sized tree has come into its own with today's smaller

gardens. Its slender dark trunk supports an intricate mass of thin branches that are well clothed with narrow silver-grey leaves. Called *salicifolia* it is not surprising that this tree is suggested by nurserymen as an alternative to the weeping willow that soon out-grows allotted space.

It forms a rounded head with a proportion of the branches arch-ing downwards. The variety *P.s.* 'Pendula' exaggerates this natural tendency. It is a good winter silhouette. In spring, when young leaves are at their most silvery, they are accompanied by white blossom and the tree becomes very special. Leaves never lose all their metallic gleam although they do become somewhat greener with age.

Quercus
There are many magnificently leaved oaks but they demand space. The scarlet oak, *Q. coccinea,* can hold its glorious vivid red leaves till Christmas, but like *Q. rubra* (red oak) which is another very splen-did brute, it reaches for the stratosphere, 23 to 25m (70 to 80ft) is easily attained.

Rhus
The sumachs, as shrubs or small trees, are grown for their foliage, though the sparingly branched design lines can appeal strongly to some gardeners and this feature may be underscored by juxtaposi-tion to overcoated conifers or well-appointed shrubs like camellias, berberis species and hybrids, or lower masses of such as the grey-leaved senecios.

R. typhina: stag's horn sumach   d   7m (20ft)
The few, upward-reaching branches divide to form a wide-topped small tree probably content to reach 5 to 7m (15 to 20ft) but able on occasion, and given time, to grow higher. Young bark is encased in a rough cover of short red hairs, a similar effect to that on the stag's horn. Leaves are an orthodox pinnate type, maybe six to twelve pairs rowing to the sides, the cox here being as large or larger than crew members. Leaflets are long, spear shapes with ser-rations. There is at least one cut-leaved form offered as 'Laciniata'.

Leaves start fresh green and rough to the touch. Bristled surfaces wear to a cleanshaven old age. Autumn brings eye-catching flaming reds and golds, one of the first signals of its arrival. They outdo the flaming colours of any bonfire, and are of unbeatable brilliance. The female will produce plume-like tight heads of tiny flowers, reddish to start with but becoming browner with age. These are held in clench-fisted salute from late summer into the winter.

The bold foliage design may be exaggerated; cut young plants to the ground and allow only one stem to grow from each pruned stump. Upright furry poles reach head height and carry leaves up to 1m (3ft) long.

Robinia

Robinias are amongst the most graceful of leguminous trees, flourishing in soils of modest or even poor quality. High living can cause them to outgrow their strength and disaster threatens as large brittle branches break away.

R.pseudoacacia: false or common acacia   d   24m (70ft)
A fast-growing upright tree with a spreading rounded head. Its pinnate leaves, 11 to 25 leaflets, are bright green and give an airy ferny feel to the whole. Most gardeners will hesitate about planting such a potentially tall tree but they can be easily seduced into installing the popular variety *R.p.*'Frisia' with its similar attractive foliage in sunshine-yellow colouring. This pleasingly shaped tree, a cloud of gold in leaf, appears not so stratospherically ambitious as the type. Watch out for the long sharp spines of the young plant, they are already red, we can do without them dripping blood.

Salix: willows

It irks me somewhat, as a *Salix* enthusiast who once had a collection of over two hundred and fifty different kinds, to admit that few of the tree species are outstanding for foliage alone. Disregarding those too large for most gardens, we are left with very few. However, one has quite outstanding foliage and another is interesting.

S.magnifica   d   3 to 7m (10 to 20ft)
This makes a shrub or small tree; casual observers could be forgiven for not identifying it as a willow. No slim-leaved character this. Its grey-green leaves could have been filched from a magnolia or a laurel. They measure from 10 to 25cm (4 to 10in) long by an opulent 7 to 15cm (3 to 6in) wide. Leaf stalks are a reddish purple and sometimes a little of this follows into the midrib. Class is added by the rich purple of the pointed stems and young wood that becomes ruby red.

S.matsudana tortuosa: the corkscrew tree   d   7 to 10m (20 to 30ft)
This grows rapidly. A 20cm (9in) cutting can be a head-high sapling in a season. This quickly establishes itself as a tree not unlike a silver birch in stature but maybe a little wider. Olive-coloured branches twist, the twigs contort in all directions, so that the winter silhouette cuts an intricate jigsaw from the sky. Raindrops hang on a thousand curled twigs and bejewel the whole. Narrow typical willow leaves of light green are themselves curled and twisted. Best where falling leaves are not going to cause too much annoyance as this is a protracted exercise.

Sambucus nigra: elder   d   5 to 7m (15 to 20ft)
Wild elder can be lovely in flower and in fruit, but it is a garden weed too quick to seed itself. However, there are two good cultivars. The golden elder, *S.n.* 'Aurea', is popular with those responsible for stocking public areas where its amenable nature is exploited by

being cut back hard each season or so. Coppiced to ground level, or grown as a shrub, it produces a strong fountain of huge, bright, lemony-gold leaves. This and *S.n.* 'Guincho Purple' are excellent garden plants and if subjected to regular cutting back cannot ever become invasive weeds. They can both make typical elder trees though the leaves are then smaller, more crowded, and lose some of the brilliance of disciplined shrubby plants.

Sassafras officinale   d   20m (60ft)
A good specimen tree as a youngster before outgrowing its space, a shapely, upright, well-clothed, widely columnar tree. Large, handsome leaves are a polished dark green more or less oval shaped and from 7 to 18cm (3 to 7in) long by 5 to 10cm (2 to 4in) wide.

Sophora japonica: Japanese pagoda tree   d   17m (50ft)
This very wide, rounded tree has a branching pattern that allows the outer branches to come close to the ground. It is one of the best leguminous trees with pinnate leaves of rich green 12 to 25cm (1 to 2ft) long with nine to fifteen oval leaflets 2 to 5cm (1 to 2in). It is just as well that it makes a pleasing foliage tree because it could be more than 20 years before it flowers with large bunches in creamy white.

Sorbus: whitebeams and rowans
The *sorbus* genus splits into the pinnate leaved rowan-like types

Rhus typhina, the stag-horn sumach, from eastern North America, a strong deciduous shrub or tree attractive in full growth and one of the earliest and most brilliant of autumn colourers *(Author)*

and the simple-leaved whitebeams. The foliage of both persuasions have their points. *S. aria* in its various whitebeam cultivars all have tough, sensible leaves, neatly serrated, more or less felty-white below, and grey-green above. They are splendid as they unfurl from their buds, luminous in silvery-white infancy, more like flowers than leaves, altogether decorative rather than utilitarian. Normally this is a neat, compact, rounded conical tree with dark trunk and branches and with leaves retaining a white cast below, but becoming rich green above as they attain adulthood. *S. a.* 'Magnifica' is the type writ bolder, larger, and with orange fruit. *S. a.* 'Majestica' has large, green leaves gleaming white below; this is one of the best cloned forms, very compact in its wide, conical shape. *S. a.* 'Lutescens' has leaves limy yellow in youth but later standard green.

The pinnate leaved are numerous. Our native mountain ash, *S. aucuparia,* displays attractive foliage and crops of orange-red fruits. The Welsh used to plant one close to the doorway to keep witches at bay. The rowan is slow growing, the form 'Edulis' *(S. a. moravica)* is stronger with large fruits. The craggy picturesque aspect of these trees is half their charm, but there can also be a place for the dense upward-reaching 'Fastigiata' with strong branches, fine foliage, and bunches of scarlet fruit. The smaller tree, 'Pendula', has characterfull spreading and then cascading branches.

Autumn leaf colours of our rowans are a lovely but fleeting sight. Some exotic relatives are even more brilliant. The Chinese *S. discolor* is easy, similar to the rowan in habit and leaf, though perhaps it is a little bolder and, in the autumn, can be the most highly coloured of all. Its berries are white, not red. *S. hupehensis* has green leaves suffused a purplish shade, colouring that is more obvious with age. It becomes bright with flame colours in the fall. White flowers are followed by pink-blushed berries. The clone 'November Pink' is particularly good with dark leaves and light-pink berries.

Sorbus vilmorinii has delicate pinnate foliage, much lighter and more graceful than most rowans

S. vilmorinii   d   3 to 7m (10 to 20ft)

I am partial to this dainty little tree. Its modest dimensions, its pleasant but undemonstrative form, and the delicate, tailored small leaves, charmingly pinnate and neatly serrated, add up to a very telling, unassuming charm. The foliar green is flushed pinky purple. Leaves are possibly the smallest and neatest of the genus. The bunches of white flowers are succeeded by persistent widely spaced berries, a rosy red to start with, but after leaf fall, turning white with a modest blush of pink.

'Joseph Rock' is a strong rowan type, rather erect and gaunt, but with a fairly compact head. Typical largish mountain ash foliage dies off in many fiery shades. Tight large bunches of gold fruits persist into winter.

Stuartia, syn. Stewartia pseudocamellia   d   7m (20ft)

Oval leaves up to 7 to 10cm (3 to 4in) long are a rich green, sometimes glabrous like the shoots, and die off in magnificent golds and reds. The name acknowledges the likeness of the open white blossoms to those of single camellia flowers. Five petals have a centre boss of stamens very much in the camellia style. The flaking bark is not the least of its charms.

Styrax japonica   d   4 to 8m (12 to 25ft)
Planted in good, drained soil with a good humus content in a position free of late spring frosts, this can be first class in small gardens. Overall grace of form with lightweight branches, sometimes arching downwards, tell heavily in its favour, though the June blossoming is also stylish and appealing. Foliage is of oval leaves painted in high gloss, green above. Hanging below the leaves, the white bell flowers make a chic picture.

The Shrubs

Shrubs are both bones and flesh of the long winter picture. They may be the main design element; numbers, sizes, diversity and beauty demand it. Balance of evergreen and deciduous determines the atmosphere year round, but especially after leaf fall. The most exciting gardens are those that make good use of both classes. Completely evergreen gardens, such as some in rhododendron country, can be a little heavy and staid outside flowering times.

By working to the dictum that 'a garden should be designed for the winter; other seasons will look after themselves', there will be little to fear. Evergreen kinds are on double time, we deploy them to the very best effect, some close at hand, some maybe breaking the bareness of brick walls; others, perhaps brighter shades, can light up the middle ground whilst patterns of colour, tone, and form draw the eye towards the rear.

Heavy-coated evergreens look all the more luxuriant when contrasted with bare stems of neighbouring deciduous kinds that can be impressive in colour or spatial design. It is wrong to ignore such easy things as the colour-barked dogwoods. The red of *Cornus alba* or one of the named clones, and the olive yellow of *C. stolonifera* 'Flaviramea' can be most effective from October till April, against conifer, evergreen viburnum, camellia or any rich greens. Cut down in spring, the dogwoods make vivid new growth for next winter but not only this, their upward-reaching energy has the excitement of the strongly vertical, contrasted with the statuesque evergreen.

The cascading lines of such as the Kilmarnock willow, *Salix caprea pendula,* seen against the golden mass of a yellow conifer, a golden variegated holly or a rampant *Elaeagnus pungens* 'Maculata', can look interesting for months before it makes its move and displays silver pussy willow buds and then golden powder puffs of scattering pollen. Then it assumes its mature grey-green foliar mantle.

A stand of *Rubus thibetanus* 'Silver Fern' looks good, an aristocrat among proletarian brambles. Upright stems are attractively clothed with much cut, pointed pinnate leaves, each perhaps composed of over a dozen leaflets in healthy glossy green, slightly silken above and rust felted below. The name 'Silver Fern' is descriptive, it looks ferny, and the stems have a silvery bloom over a purple undercoat, a telling winter effect.

Lots of smaller conifers, such as *Thuja occidentalis* 'Rheingold', that after a long time may become a tree, spend most of their lives in shrubby proportions. 'Rheingold' is popular because of its dense golden cover to the ground, its even, wide conical form, and its winter appearance when it looks even better with warm shades of rusty orange. Junipers in their varying stages of prostration are excellent value, useful in awkward spots and with good blues,

Shrubs

silvers, greens, and golds. Definite design lines help build interesting cameos within the garden.

Outreaching branches of healthily clad golden-green *Juniperus x media* 'Pfitzeriana Aurea' makes it a garden classic, but it is all the more telling close to some cloud-shaped dark mass such as *Viburnum tinus*. Polished-leaved camellias might be another possibility; one foregoes the winter posies of the viburnum but the lacquered dark leaves of such as the popular *Camellia x williamsii* 'Donation' can be an eloquent contrast to the glittery look of the juniper, its small leafy and stemmy bits fragmenting the light falling on it.

Thought is needed about winter design. There needs to be low prostrate plants like heathers and flat junipers, plenty of rounded and bushy items both evergreen and deciduous because we wish to enjoy their splendid leaves and blossom. What we should remember is that the vertical is most important. Horizontal lines engender feelings of peace. Criss-crossing lines create an atmosphere of intrigue, conflict and excitement. Upright lines give a sense of reaching and of energy. Trees reach for the sky, but even at shrub level those that point definitely upward give an impression of purpose that laxer shapes cannot manage. A tall bamboo clump mid-lawn is bold, keeping tedium and mediocrity at bay.

Colour Charts

Varying forms and sizes give variety; leaf shapes and sizes build up the mosaic, but our eyes register first the colours. Some leaves are green: vast numbers are yellow, silver, bronze, red, or purple. Even those thought of as green may well have an admixture of other colours even if not so obvious as variegation. Some very plain mid-year leaves are excitingly coloured in youth and again in old age. Individuals will receive praise and blame in review, here some are shortlisted by their predominant colour:

Golden

Acer cappadocicum 'Aureum'
   japonicum 'Aureum'
   negundo 'Aureovariegatum'
Chamaecyparis lawsoniana
   'Lutea' + vars
Cupressus macrocarpa 'Goldcrest'
Juniperus chinensis 'Aurea'

Ligustrum ovalifolium 'Aureum'
Lonicera nitida 'Baggesen's Gold'
Philadelphus coronarius 'Aureus'
   + vars
Ribes alpinum 'Aureum'
   sanguineum 'Brocklebankii'
Weigela florida 'Aureovariegata'

Silver blue grey

Artemisia arborescens
Atriplex halimus
Caryopteris x clandonesis
Cistus 'Silver Pink'
Cytisus battandieri
Eleaegnus angustifolia
   argentea (commutata)
Eucalyptus, many

Hebe albicans
   colensoi
   pinguifolia 'Pagei'
Salix lanata
   repens argentea
Santolina chamaecyparissus
   neapolitana
Senecio 'Sunshine'

Berberis thunbergii
'Harlequin' is one of the most
entertaining of the many
coloured forms of the
species. Background colour
of burgundy splashed with
pink and cream

Red and orange
Acer palmatum
Berberis thundergii in vars
Calluna in vars
Photinia glabra 'Rubens'

Photinia fraseri 'Red Robin' + vars
Pieris 'Firecrest' + vars
Prunus cerasifera 'Hollywood'

Purple and maroon
Acer campestre 'Schwerinii' + vars
Berberis gagnepainii 'Purpurea'
   interposita 'Wallich Purple'
   thunbergii 'Dart's Purple'
   + vars
Betula pendula 'Purpurea'

Corylus maxima 'Purpurea'
Cotinus coggygria 'Royal Purple'
Prunus cerasifera in vars
   x cistena 'Crimson Dwarf
   spinosa 'Purpurea'
Rosa rubrifolia

Autumnal Colour
Acers listed here will often make trees, but this takes many years.

Acer campestre
   circinatum
   cissifolium
   griseum
   henryi
   japonicum
   nikoense
   palmatum
   tschonoskii
Amelanchier canadensis
Berberis concinna
   koreana
   x mentorensis
   thunbergii in vars
   vulgaris
   wilsoniae
   yunnanensis
Carya ovata (alba)
Cercidiphyllum japonicum

Cladastris tinctoria
Cotinus coggygria
Enkianthus in var
Euonymus alatus
   latifolius
Fothergilla gardenii
   (alnifolia)
Oxydendrum arboreum
Prunus incisa + small species
Ribes americanum
Spiraea thunbergii
Vaccinium alnifolium
Viburnum alnifolium
   opulus in var
Zelkova as a shrub
   carpinifolia
   serrata

The Variegated
For some, the variegated are outside the law. In the sunny days of youth I was agin the government and agin the variegated. I am still at odds with the government but now good-quality variegated plants are welcomed.

It is wise to look twice at new variegated plants as many are unfortunate accidents, but we would be much the poorer without the better variegated hollies and the eleagnus types to brighten up the garden, especially in winter. Some to consider are these:

Aralia elata 'Variegata'
   elata 'Aureovariegata'
Aucuba japonica in var
Cornus alba 'Elegantissima'

Euonymus fortunei in var
Hedera in var
Ilex in var
Osmanthus heterophyllus in var

alba 'Spaethii'   *Vinca* in var
Elaeagnus ebbingei in var
  pungens in var

Acer

Maples are frontrunners in the foliar stakes. Brightly coloured as
they open, they are mainly very pleasant through the year, and die
off with a crescendo of brilliance. Many, capable of making reasonably sized trees, are slow growing shrubs for a long time. You could
fill a fine garden with nothing but acers.

A.circinatum: vine maple   d   3+m (10ft+)
Although gardeners may dragoon this to form a trunk that can eventually support a tree as high as a house, if left alone it makes a
thickety spreading shrub that can be the centre of attention early in
the year as leaves begin to emerge from buds and flowers open.
Sprays of flowers are a mix of small whitish petals and burgundy
sepals. Leaf scales are as decorative in glistening crimson. Leaves are
green 7 to 12cm (3 to 5in) wide and as long, the five or seven
pointed lobes suggesting the shape of vine leaves. They become
orange and red in the autumn.

    Some acers, like the more delicately coloured *A.palmatum*
kinds, enjoy some shading from the sun and protection from late
spring frosts. *A. circinatum* is not so 'nesh', it will make a distinctive
specimen in the border or alone in the lawn. The one or two named
forms include the compact 'Little Gem.'

Evergreen dense-foliaged
spreading shrubs: green-and-
white *Euonymus fortunei*
'Emerald Gaiety', and gold-
and-green *E.f.* 'Emerald 'N'
Gold'

A.griseum   d   10m (30ft+)

Of the group of acers that divide their leaves into three leaflets this is
the best known, a reflection of its interesting character. Whilst
really a tree, it takes its time to achieve this. Boldly serrated leaflets
can be 3 to 6cm (1½ to 2½in) long and not more than half as wide.
Whilst healthy green in the working months; come autumn they
don glad rags of reds and oranges. Since its introduction at the
beginning of the century it has been popular for the decorative flaking bark that allows the warm orange new bark to be displayed.

A.japonicum   d   7m (20ft)

This is a steady grower making a well-branched shrub and then a
tree. Its leaves are 4 to 12cm (2 to 5in) long with the basic blade
round but with five to eleven pointed lobes. It is more often seen in
its golden-leaved form, 'Aureum'. The well-displayed foliage is a
shining primrose gold, brighter than the flowers of many other
shrubs and a colour that it maintains through the summer until
autumn. 'Aconitifolium' has bright green leaves very deeply cut
giving it a ferny effect; autumn colour is red.

A.palmatum: Japanese maple   d   3 to 7m (15 to 22ft)

There can be few plants with foliage so variable in form and colour.
They are much prized in Japan, their country of origin. I do not
know how many kinds are available there, but in Britain more than
150 can be found in catalogues. You may care to raise your own
from seed which, although a slow process, will give still more
variety; every seedling seems different. The basic leaf is 5 to 10cm
(2 to 4in) wide and long, with five or seven lobes. Here are some of
the more popular offerings:

'Atropurpureum' is very rich crimson with the slightest admixture of copper, but the new shoots and leaves are shining scarlet. 'Bloodgood' produces very dark purple-red foliage that can be
used dramatically with green- and yellow-leaved kinds. Many cultivars were given Latin names so there are a series called *A.p.dissec-
tum*, ones whose leaves are finely and very deeply cut, a light ferny
feeling being achieved. *A.p. dissectum* or *A.p.* 'Dissectum Viridis'
have this finely divided foliage in bright green. As the shrub has a
more or less horizontal branching habit, the greenery is displayed
most attractively. Of similar spreading form is *A.p.* 'Dissectum
Atropurpureum' with purple-red intricately cut filigree leaves that
die off brilliantly. 'Crimson Queen' is stronger than the dark *A.p.*
'Dissectum Nigrum'. 'Inaba Shidare' varies the colour, a bronzy red.
One of the most famous of all cultivars and still highly thought of is
'Osakazuki', an upright grower in bright green that becomes brilliant in autumn oranges and reds.

Aesculus parviflora   d   2.5 to 3m (8 to 10ft)

A small relative of the horse chestnut, this attractive spreading
shrub is extremely bold, conjuring up a series of narrow, upright
stems but continuing to sucker all round to make a graceful

A marriage of form and contrast of colour. Two deeply cut-leaved forms of *Acer palmatum*: 'Dissectum Atropurpureum' (left) and 'Dissectum Viridis' *(RHS Wisley)*

rounded entity. Leaves are the horse chestnut pinnate form, five leaflets 7 to 25cm (3 to 10in) long to each leaf. It blooms freely in midsummer with lots of upright panicles of white flowers made more attractive by the striking pink stamens, carrying red anthers. Its tidy aspect and trustworthy hardiness make it one of the best of American imports, this one from the south-east. It ends the season in rich gold shades.

Agave parryi   e   50cms (1 to 2ft)

This succulent piece of pseudostatuary will please those with a liking for the unusual. Thick fleshy leaves are each as thick as an arm; together they make a rosette perhaps 75cm (2ft) across. Each leaf ends with a sharp spine and the edges are armed as well. Colours are shades of dull grey and green. It makes an interesting conversation piece, hardy in warmer parts of the country. Eventually it may send up a flower mast some 2.5 to 4m (7 to 12ft) high with a metre-long panicle of creamy bloom. This is the time to call in friends to witness what is the swansong of the agave. There are unlikely to be many such pretexts for a wake-party as agaves can live for up to 50 years before deciding to call it a day.

Amelanchier canadensis   d   7m (20+)

Leaves of this shrub are ordinary oval jobs 3 to 7cm (1½ to 3in) long. They are smothered behind a sheet of simple white flowers for a day and a half in April. The show quickly over, the foliage maintains a sensible cover until in autumn it begins to change into a variety of golds or pinky reds. At this season it is one of the most eye-catching plants in the garden. Makes a small tree.

Atriplex halimus: tree purslane   d/e   1 to 3m (3 to 8ft)

Grown for its foliage, a strong-growing shrub of open rounded aspect. Best against some dark background and then will appear to be a cloud of silver. Pointed leaves are 1 to 6cm (½ to 2½in) long and give their silvery effect because of the scaly covering. Other species are of lesser use and beauty.

Aucuba japonica   e   2 to 3m (6 to 9ft)

'Spotted laurel' is a useful legacy from the Victorians. Because they used maybe too much, a reaction set in against its proletarian virtues. Now it is taking its place again. This useful plant will grow almost anywhere. It tolerates shade, even under a deep canopy where other plants would give up the ghost. The type with tough all-green leaves is available and so are up to twenty variations, mostly with patterns of yellow spotting on the leaves similar to the standard 'Maculata' and the popular 'Variegata'. The females bear large round red berries in good numbers. The polished tough leaves 7 to 22cm (3 to 9in) make a handsome picture.

Berberis

This polymorphic genus teases the botanist and is not fully appreciated by the gardener, although the evergreen *B.darwinii* and the hybrid *B.x.stenophylla* are well known and liked.

B.aristata   d   3m (10ft)

Strong graceful spreading shrub busy with new suckering growths. Neat oval leaves grouped up to half a dozen at each node. The green dies off with good colours in autumn. Much golden blossom is succeeded by long bunches of berries that are a red overlaid by a thick blue-white bloom. Given its head it makes an impressive fountain of growth and, although basically deciduous, new growth in the flush of youth will retain leaves throughout winter.

B.calliantha   e   1m (3ft)

Attractive in its compact low growth of highly polished, miniature holly leaves, rich green above and silver white below. Foliage is distinctive and in a higher class than many other worthy berberises; individual leaves can be 3 to 8cm (1½ to 2½in) long and half as wide. Some die off each year, becoming rich orange or red and thus creating a pleasing lively pattern of colour, augmented in the spring by a modicum of pale-yellow flowers and a later scatter of almost black berries made less funereal by their grey bloom. It will often only grow 38 to 45cm (15 to 18in) high but much wider.

B.darwinii   e   2 to 3m (6 to 10ft)
Thickets of upright and arching stems are well clothed with small
dark leaves, making an ideal backcloth for the million tight clasped
flowers in rich gold or tangerine. Best planted in sheltered spots as a
real bout of hard frosts can cut back the plant dramatically.
See *B.x stenophylla.*

B.gagnepainii lanceifolia   e   2 to 3m (6 to 9ft)
Tight masses of stems create neat upright bushes of very narrow
tough leaves 3 to 10cm (1 1/2 to 4in) long but only a miniscule 2mm
(1/8in) wide. Its strong suckering needs keeping in check. Black-
green foliage highlights scattered clusters of shining yellow
blossom. In dark corners it may look nondescript; against light-
coloured senecios and such like it can look distinguished, dark
cloaked and not without theatrical presence.

B.hakeoides   e   4m (12ft)
Somewhat upright and gangling but most attractive in its leaves.
These can be 1 to 7cm (1/2 to 3in) long and wide. They are round
but regularly set with spines. At the growing end of the stems these
leaves, usually in pairs, are clasped tight into the wood but the lower
down they are the larger they become, being held on short stalks
with the lowest becoming up to 5cm (2in) long. It is a shrub to
place behind others with neater habits. Bright in early spring with
trim sprays of golden blossom held as posies with each group of
leaves.

B.linearifolia   e   1 to 3m (3 to 9ft)
A first-class shrub that to begin with may seem stiff and erect, but as
it ages this strong vertical theme, whilst not lost, is softened by laxer
branches. It is evergreen, in very rich dark green and well polished.
Although each leaf ends with a spiny point it is not one of the bel-
ligerent berberis. The flowers are large (for a berberis) and long
lasting, a blend of golden orange and orange red. A fine species,
strong, rich in narrow foliage, and brilliant in blossom. The fine
hybrid 'Orange King' has heavy crops of large vivid flowers.

B.x stenophylla   e   2 to 3m (6 to 10ft)
The original hybrid between *B.darwinii* and *B.empetrifolia* proved
hardier than *B.darwinii* and has tended to eclipse its parents. The
hybrid makes a robust thicket of upright stems with lots of secondary gracefully arching ones. All is generously clothed with small,
dark green, teethed leaves, a strong overall effect and really more
pleasing in form than either parent. In the late spring its arching
stems are laden with golden blossom. Other good varieties include
'Autumnalis' which manages both a spring and an autumn flower
display, and 'Crawley Gem' and 'Irwinii', two dwarf kinds with similar flowers and leaves.

B.thunbergii   d   60cm to 3m (2 to 9ft)

Indispensable, with different forms. Some are tall and strong for use as decorative hedges, others are unusually coloured for special places, while others are dwarf for the rock garden or where things miniature are needed.

The basic species is a neat, green-leaved plant that grows strongly upright but with plenty of arching stems to create a pleasing, graceful shape. The leaves of this and all types are very colourful in autumn, assuming deep orange and red colours. The green-leaved type is rarely seen, as purple-red ones are so popular. 'Atropurpurea' came first, a vigorous mass of richly painted foliage, followed by 'Atropurpurea Nana', compact and small enough for some rock gardens. 'Bagatelle' is compact, also with mahogany-red leaves turning strong crimson in the autumn. 'Harlequin' is a neat small-leaved form with rosy purple leaves speckled white or cream. 'Red Chief' has some of the most striking of all foliage, dressed in rich red leaves from strong upright and arching branches. Some cultivars are of spreading habit, 'Green Carpet' is bright and might well feature as a ground-cover plant. It decorates itself with modest yellow blossom and more noticeable crops of narrow, oval, red shiny fruits.

B.verruculosa   e   1 to 2m (3 to 6ft)

Tough, neat, dwarf hedgehog-like shrub in dark green. Well-polished foliage, brown stems with thin spines, and yellow flowers.

B.wilsoniae   e/d   1 to 2m (3 to 6ft)

Spreading, arching branches add grace to a basically tight shrub with grey-green foliage. The foliage becomes orange-red in autumn and, though much may fall, a proportion will often see the winter through. The small lemony flowers are followed by fruits, pinky-red, frosted, glass beads.

Buddleja alternifolia   d   3 to 4m (10 to 12ft)

This is better than many buddlejas in its foliage. It makes a shrub or small tree with lots of long, slender branches that fall soilwards. These are well clothed with alternately arranged long, pointed leaves silvered in youth with down. Whilst this wears off with age, the leaves never lose all their metallic look. *B.a.* 'Argentea' has an enhanced silveriness that is more lasting. To grow it as a tree will need the gardener's help by support and surgery; alone it makes a pleasing enough hump of cascading branches but as a small tree, perhaps more than 3m (10ft) tall, it is outstanding. It can upstage a weeping willow, and this in a silvery grey that can be spotlighted by dark holly or yew behind. In June every leaf axil seems to hold its own tightly arranged rounded posy of lilac flowers, so many that the long pendant branches can be enwreathed their whole lengths. Recommended as easy on good soils.

Other buddlejas are not without points. The popular *B.davidii* cultivars (butterfly bushes) are mainly large-leaved strong-growing plants with big, long, rather rough grey-green leaves. 'Nanho Blue' is promoted as a dwarf; on some garden centre labels a height of 1m (3 to 4ft) is given — this is nonsense. The plants will grow to 1.5m (5ft) in their first season, but it is a smaller, more graceful bush than the larger relatives and is easily managed. It makes a fountain of upward and arching strong stems with plenty spreading down below so that there is no danger of a gawky bush. The leaves are grey-green. The autumn will see the large mature leaves fall and the shrub left with branches almost bare — almost but not quite, as it is decorated with small young leaves arranged like rosettes that gleam silver grey through much of the winter. The flowers are long, graceful, purplish-blue pointed cones.

Buxus: box   e   1 to 7m (3 to 20ft)
Box is still used as an edging plant, as mini-hedges, and in corners where very little else will survive. Apart from the virtues of hardiness, evergreen colour, and topiarian value, to my mind it lacks distinction.

Calluna: see chapter on ground cover.

Camellia
Where these grow well they can be amongst the best of foliage shrubs. Their forte is the conventional plain leaf-shaped leaf in rich green, all highly lacquered. Leastways the *C.japonica* and the *C.x williamsii* hybrids conform to this specification, the *C.reticulata* brood have similar leaves, oval, tough, and dark green, but have duller surfaces marked by reticulate veinwork.

The winter foliage of *Buddleja nanhoensis* 'Nanho Blue' has attractive miniaturised silvery leaves. In midsummer opulence it is much less coarse than the popular *B.davidii* cultivars

Camellias are lovers of peaty soil but will grow perfectly well in ordinary garden soil with an admixture of peat or leaf mould especially in their younger years. They object to lime which causes them to become yellow and then to die.

Corylus maxima: hazel (filbert)   d   3 to 7m (9 to 20ft)

This is much the same as the common hazel but is writ bolder. It grows strongly with large hazel leaves and typical hazel catkins and nuts. It has an outstanding variety, the purple-leaved 'Purpurea' with leaves of very dark maroon purple. Once a plant is established, if it is coppiced every two or so seasons, it will produce strong, upright growth furnished with leaves two or three times the standard-sized ones; a length of 18cm (7in) is entirely possible. They gain their best colour in full light, another reason for cutting the bush back.

Cotoneaster

It is difficult to point to any species whose foliage is outstanding and impossible to point to any whose foliage is poor. Of the larger kinds *C.frigidus* has good tough dark oval leaves, and *C.x watererii* is equally impressive. Ground-covering *C.dammerii* hybrids are energetic workers. 'Eichholz' makes a good cover with rich, green leaves that have a blue cast. Red berries are freely borne.

Cotoneaster watererii, capable of making a small tree (top); *C.borizontalis*, the popular shrub for covering the first few feet of walls (left); and *C.dammerii* 'Skogholm', one of the ground-hugging types

Cytisus battandierii   e   2 to 3m (6 to 9ft)

What a broom this is! Some of the small species are quite useful foliage plants but the green stems make as much impact as the smallish leaves. It makes little sense to compare *C.battandierii* with other species, it is so much larger in all its parts. In cold areas it is best grown against a wall, but in many places it can be grown easily in the open and will not seem to miss its native Moroccan heat. It is a sun lover, like all brooms. The large, evergreen leaves are silver grey, the effect of silken hairs over the leaf surfaces. Leaves are pinnate like most leguminous plants; individual leaflets are oval and measure up to 7cm (3in) long. Prolonged frosts may cause it to drop leaves but the weather has to be very severe to do this. The pea flowers are gathered together in upright cones that smell of pine-apples. It grows quickly but, like orthodox brooms, is not particu-larly long lived. A youngster will soon be above head height and will normally end up being twice as wide as tall. The metallic sheen of the foliage is unusual in leaves of this form.

Deutzia scabra   d   3m (10ft)

The genus is not often thought of as leading foliage plants but this one is not without appeal. It is often grown as the double-flowered 'Plena'. Strong stems are well endowed with smooth, clean, green ovate leaves and the obvious good health of these together with their very neat arrangement make this a stylish bush, especially if lesser stems are cut back and older parts are thinned regularly. New strong growth has good leaf cover.

Elaeagnus

This is almost exclusively grown for foliar beauty, the flowers being regarded as irrelevant. Some are deciduous like *E.angustifolia* and *E.commutata (argentea)* and will grow well on poor sandy soils, when their leaves seem to be at their most heavily silvered. Others that are evergreen include some useful garden plants like the golden-leaved variegated *E.pungens* 'Maculata', which can bring sunshine into the dullest day.

E.commutata (argentea): silver berry   d   2 to 4m (5 to 12ft)

Whilst *E.angustifolia* is a splendid shrub or small tree with white stems and grey leaves shining white below, it is beaten by the purer metal of the silver berry. This makes a stand of upright, slender stems from a suckering base. Younger stems are covered with shiny red-brown scales, a contrast to the leaves whose top and bottom surfaces are overlaid with silver scales. The silvered foliage alone makes an attractive picture, especially if stationed in front of a dark neighbour, but it also produces lots of similarly silvered buds that open as little four-pointed flowers dispensing a sweet fragrance. Then, as if that were not enough, oval berries are added in matching silverwork.

E.pungens (E.p.aureo-variegata)   e   4m (12ft+)

This hardy, spreading shrub, thick with abundant foliage, is grown
in several forms. Some are decidedly more attractive than others.
'Goldrim' is a healthy kind with bright golden variegation around
the leaf margins. Most popular of all is *E.p.* 'Maculata' in which the
centre of the leaf is given over to the gold and, in most, quite narrow
margins are left deep green. The variegation varies and odd shoots
will revert to pure green but it is no hardship to cut these away. The
plant deserves its popularity because it has abundant vigour, glowing colour, and a high gloss finish.

X Fatshedera lizei   e   2m (5ft)

The handsome foliage of this interesting plant gives some indication
of its parentage as does its general demeanour. It is one of those
rarities, a bigeneric hybrid, the result of the mating of *Fatsia
japonica* 'Moseri' and *Hedera helix* 'Hibernica'. Great polished
leaves are made of heavy calibre material and can be as much as
25cm (10in) across, though they are not quite as long. They are five
lobed in the palmate fashion of the fatsia. Unlike the fatsia, this
hybrid has some of the ivy's sprawling manner and it needs support
for a year or two until it establishes a bit of backbone. It then forms a
shrub of abundant vigour, more informal in its disposition than the
fatsia. It is very hardy and can do well in areas that get little light.
Here its foliage can be opulent, converting a third-rate site into one
of interest and beauty. Flowers come at the end of the growing year

and form one of the few flowering points in the November garden. Rounded umbels of 10-40 flowers are a pattern of greenish cream.

Fatsia japonica   e   2 to 4m (6 to 12ft)

Whilst enjoying a long and successful career as a pot plant this most handsome of foliage plants is not seen outside as often as its value deserves. It makes a relatively sparingly branched, sturdy, rounded bush but the lack of branching wood is no matter because it is so well furnished with the largest natural leaves of any evergreen in the garden. These are palmate arrangements, huge hands with perhaps nine pointed fingers all in rich green kept highly polished. They can be 30 to 45cm (12 to 18in) across. Rounded heads of creamy-white flowers, rather on the same design as those of ivies, are a decorative feature in October through to December. Will grow well in shade.

Ficus carica: fig   d   2 to 3m (6 to 9ft)

In very mild spots the fig can be grown in the open, but more often it needs a sunny wall where, even if cut back by prolonged spine-chilling weather, it will grow again from the base to form its skeleton of grey branches from which to display the attractive rough leaves as wide as long, measuring 10 to 20cm (4 to 8in). With three or five shallow rounded lobes they are distinctive, their bristled surfaces making their green somewhat greyish. The tiny flowers are followed by fruits that, started one year, may or may not develop fit to eat the next.

Fothergilla major   d   2 to 3m (6 to 9ft)

The relationship to the witch-hazels *Hamamelis* is borne out by steady rate of growth, the branching habit, and the leaves. These are more rounded than oval and 5 to 10cm (2 to 4in) long, but are smoother and more polished than the witch-hazel's. It enjoys some leaf mould or peat in the soil and will then make a pleasing shrub, well dressed with leaves and with two seasons of especial interest. In May it produces petal-less flowers, rounded arrangements of pinky-white stamens finished with yellow-pollened anthers. These many domes are from 2 to 5cm (1 to 2in) across and make the shrub festive in an unusual way. Then, come the autumn, it vies with neighbours in the decorative value of its autumn colours, golds and golden oranges.

Garrya elliptica   e   2 to 4m (5 to 12ft)

The long winter tassel catkins of this shrub will plead for its admission to the garden. It is obviously worth its place in winter; what is more open to debate is its value during the rest of the year. Its dense mass of tough, very dark green leaves are somewhat dull and there is no autumn colour when the leaves die. It is best planted amongst cheerful, light-coloured types where its solemnity may add contrast.

Gaultheria shallon   e   75cm to 2 m (2 to 5ft)

Wet, dark places are not popular with many plants but although this will not demand such conditions, it will thrive in such an area. It increases by vigorous suckering to form a wide mass of growth, an evergreen ensemble of tough, oval leaves 3 to 10cm (1 ½ to 4in) long.

Hebe

This huge family ranges from minute to sizeable bushes growing as much as 2m (6ft) high. They vary also in their hardiness. Many are tough, others can be killed quite easily by hard frosts.

H.brachysiphon   e   1.5m (5ft)

This is a neat species of a neat-growing genus. It makes an even rounded bush as much as twice wider than tall. The full, green, oval leaves are mounted almost touching, like a pile of plates. It makes almost every other shrub look untidy or at least informal. It is worth growing as a foliage shrub and looks as good when small as it does when mature. It provides a generous floral effort towards the end of summer when few other shrubs so exercise themselves. Then the bush is covered with neat 5cm (2in) long, cone-shaped masses of small white flowers.

H.cupressoides   e   50cm to 1m (18in to 3ft)

Not much exercise of the imagination was needed for the specific name, its impersonation of a young cupressus or juniper is saucily accurate. From the newly purchased small plant, as big as a tennis ball, until it becomes a metre — three feet — or more high, it maintains a rounded intricate mass of twigs so well clothed, slightly greyish but yellowish at the growing tips, that few people will believe it is not a conifer of any kind. It is usually much wider than tall.

Hardy hebes: the bright-green upright *Hebe rakaiensis*, the spreading grey *H.pinguifolia* 'Pagei', and the grey *H.pinguifolia*, sometimes suffused with wine colours

H.ochracea (H.armstrongii)   e   30 to 90cm (12 to 30in)

The small leaves of this plant are close pressed to the stems and, like the last, it looks coniferous. It makes a spreading shrub of unusual yellow-brown colouring (khaki sounds unlovely but is quite accurate), the stems and leaves are uniformly coloured and in all the effect is bright. Some of the twigs will be arranged in a fanned plane, rather like many conifers. It is now usually offered as the clone 'James Stirling' a good, vigorous, low one.

H.pinguifolia   e   30cm to 1m (1 to 3ft)

Our clone is one that makes a steadily increasing, neat bush, three times wider than tall and with many upright sturdy stems neatly furnished with a succession of firm, oval leaves of grey-green. These are disposed along the stems in four closely dressed ranks. Young leaves are pencil margined with a pinky mauve and are similarly gently flushed on the under-surfaces that are displayed in the fat leaf buds at the ends of all the many stems. There is a period in spring when this flush of pinky purple invades the leaves more strongly and adds extra interest to the plant. The widespread 'Pagei' is more spreading, forming wide mats of low foliage, smaller by almost half, at a maximum of 1cm (½in) long. It is a grey white.

Mahonia aquifolium is a good foliage plant although sometimes gets treated as a poor relation to species such as *M.japonica*. Dark evergreen lacquered foliage is often purpled, especially in the cooler months, and they may turn fiery red before dying

Itea virginica
d   1 to 2m (3 to 5ft)

Listed as deciduous, it can hold its bright green oval leaves until Christmas. It grows easily and increases its dimensions in similar fashion to the deutzias and philadelphus, which are cousins. Healthy foliage cover is made of leaves 3 to 9cm (1½ to 3½in) long and half as wide. Fragrant flowers open in July and August to decorate it with white bottle-brush blooms 8 to 15cm (3 to 6in) long. Other iteas are attractive but not hardy.

Leucothoe

An ericaceous lime-hating genus. They are a handsome lot, though not all are hardy. *L.fontanesiana (catesbaei)* and *L.keiskei* pass the test of our winters. The first is easily the most popular. It makes a plant 75cm to 2m (2 to 5ft) high with long, erratically wandering arching stems furnished with shining, dark oval leaves each drawn out to a long point. Lots of hanging racemes are tightly crowded with typical heather flowers in white. There is a popular variegated form in green, cream, yellow, and pink. This is 'Rainbow' with a more pleasing medley of variegation than on some other plants. *L. keiskei* is a 1m (3ft) high species with young stems and red foliage. Leaves are of the same shape as the last, individual white flowers are larger.

Ligustrum lucidum
e   3 to 4m (9 to 12ft)

Yes, this is a privet, but a superior one. In full growth it has a glow of health, the oval leaves a highly polished, shining green. Shoot ends bear large white panicles of bloom, erect, and 15 to 22cm (6 to 9in) long and almost as wide. This is in autumn when a lack of flowers makes its contribution doubly welcome. The dark foliage of *L.japonicum* can be a pleasing contrast to others such as the golden privet, *L.ovalifolium* 'Aureum', which could be the most popular of all variegated plants.

Mahonia

Some of the most distinctively leaved shrubs belong to this fine genus. The common *M. aquifolium* is not to be despised, with flattened holly foliage in dark green often becoming red or reddish-purple in winter. Its suckering habit may need checking or it might be allowed freedom where it does not matter how far it strays to make a ground cover some 1 to 2m (30in to 6ft) high. 'Atropurpurea' has good, deep red-purple foliage in winter.

M. bealei   e   2 to 3m (6 to 9ft)

An erect sturdy shrub with, eventually, several upright stems furnished with large, distinctive, pinnate leaves held horizontally. Leaves can be considerable, perhaps 60cm (2ft) long and of many pairs of leaflets each up to 15cm (6in) long. Their blue green has a narrow, tough, paler margin with spiny teeth and at the base of each leaflet there is a pale yellowish spot, a quick diagnostic help to differentiate it from *M.japonica*. Pointed clusters of lemon-yellow flowers appear as the winter advances.

Philadelphus coronarius 'Aureus' is grown for its healthy bright-yellow foliage rather than the small scented white flowers. It is brightest in the first half of its year, and is shown off to perfection here against the dark-green and red *Photina* x *fraserii* 'Red Robin'

M.japonica   e   2 to 3m (6 to 9ft)
Another upright shrub with several firm stems topped by flat
pinnate leaves, rather like a miniature palm tree. They are tough,
teethed, and a yellowish green. Winter bunches of primrose-yellow
flowers are fragrant. This, crossed with the somewhat tender
M.lomariifolia, gave fine hybrids.

Widest-grown hybrid is 'Charity' vigorously making an erect
shrub with several unbranched stems topped with handsome pinnate leaves of six or more pairs of leaflets. These are long oval shapes
brought to a sharp point. Several 15 to 25cm (6 to 10in) spikes of
lemon bells appear at the end of each stem in the winter and will last
for weeks. On milder days their distinct lemony perfume can be
detected. Whilst the spikes of 'Charity' tend to point sideways, those
of the rather similar 'Winter Sun', which opens a little later, point
more directly upright. A proportion of leaves will drop each year
and these can take on interesting shades or orange red before
falling. 'Lionel Fortesque' is particularly prolific in November and
December, lasting in good order for weeks with large heads of long
upward-pointing sprays of golden-lemon flowers. It makes an erect
bush but puts on plenty of middle-age spread by producing a succession of stems. Foliage is the standard fanned-out, flat holly shapes
in clean mid-green.

Osmanthus heterophyllus (O.aquifolium)   e   2 to 3m (6 to 9ft)
It looks like a holly, although its leaves are arranged oppositely not

Mahonia japonica, with its
handsome evergreen foliage
as tough as holly, but longer
spined and flatter

alternately, and it certainly rivals the holly as one of the best of evergreen plants. It is formidable, with thick rounded well-clothed masses of highly polished, dark green, teethed, tough leaves. Each is 3 to 6cm (1½ to 2½in) long and not so wide. Adult leaves at the top of a mature tree can have entire margins with not a prickle in sight. However it takes many years to grow this big. Minute posies of tiny white flowers are produced in the autumn and these are sweet scented. There are variegated forms, some favour gold and others are more silvery. *O.h.* 'Variegatus' has creamy-white leaf margins.

Philadelphus coronarius 'Aureus'   d   3 to 4m (9 to 12ft)
Typically easy mock orange growth, this blooms in June but is florally outshone by the hybrids. Foliage is especially good through the spring in the first flush of golden youth. As the summer arrives the gold is a little adulterated with green. Pruning back older branches in winter can encourage fresh new growth and bright foliage.

Pieris
These shrubs are grand cousins of the heathers. They hate lime and are shrubs that bloom freely but are elegant in foliage at all times.

P.floribunda   e   1 to 2m (3 to 6ft)
A spreading wide shrub of rounded form, with dark-green polished leaves of pointed oval form 4 to 8cm (1½ to 3in) long but only about a third the width. Slow-growing bushes of neat conformation, they have heather-shaped white flowers in four or so upright panicles up to 12cm (5in) long at the end of each stem. They start opening in early spring, perhaps March, and last into April. It will help if they can be sheltered from wind and frost.

P.formosa forrestii   e   2 to 3m (6 to 9ft)
A fine shrub of more upright stance than the last. The very dark-green leaves are a little larger than those of *P.floribunda.* Early on comes young foliage in shining shades of salmon, oranges, and reds, more spectacular than many flowering plants and most bewitching on a large specimen. Terminal flower panicles have been prepared in the autumn and open towards the end of March or into April. These are of large white flowers, hung on many stems, perhaps 15cm (6in) long. Young foliage colour lasts well, then goes through a succession of pinky-yellow shades before becoming green and forming part of the established order. There are especially good named forms. 'Wakehurst' is one rich-coloured one. 'Forest Flame' is probably the most widely grown, one of the finest of foliage plants. It is well named, as the young leaves are a fiery red in the spring. The colour then changes through a hundred subtle shades to pinks, cream and finally green.

P.japonica   e   3m (9ft)
A shrub of wide form and clothed to the soil with branches full of neat, narrow, tough, polished leaves. Early spring displays are of

Pittosporum tenuifolium
'Purpureum', dark as a deep
copper beech, and *Skimmia
japonica* a very neat
evergreen with red berries
most of the year

Rhododendron

good-sized heather flowers, in many quite long, dropping panicles from every twig end. In this it is perhaps more graceful than some of its relatives. The flower colour may be white, blush pink, or a rosy pink. Names of forms will probably tell flower colour. 'Purity' is a rather tighter growing form than most, with unblemished white flowers. 'Christmas Cheer' and 'Valley Rose' are two early flowering rosy kinds. They have beautifully coloured young foliage, particularly fine in 'Select', a shapely bush with lots of flowers and lacquered bronzed young leaves.

P.taiwanensis   e   2 to 3m (6 to 9ft)

With narrower foliage than *P.formosa* and more erect flowers than *P.japonica,* it looks like a slimline version. It is very pleasing when young and when established. The dark, long, spear-shaped leaves are lightened by the delicate young leaves in all shades of orange, pink, and cream. The flowers, on standby since autumn, open pure white in April with lots hanging from longish panicles, smaller than their relatives but hardly less showy.

Pittosporum tenuifolium   e   7m (20+ft)

Pittosporums are used commercially for their cut foliage. They grow most readily in the southwest where several of these antipodean species flourish. *P.tenuifolium* is usually safe anywhere; it is the hardiest of the lot and has given rise to a series of varieties. Leaves are about as big as a privet's but tougher. The margins are entire but often waved so that light plays on them. Colour is variable, the type is a good mid-green, but some like *P.t.* 'Atropurpureum' have dark chocolate-purple leaves, others are coloured either overall or by variegation with greater or lesser amounts of yellow, gold or cream. Size is another variable; there is a small 'Tom Thumb' cultivar, but most can grow into small trees. This is far more likely in Cornwall and near the Gulf Stream. Plants are amenable to pruning and can be kept as shapely specimens of around 1m (3ft) or less, if so desired. Different coloured forms look well in a group.

Pyracantha

Firethorns are grown for their huge crops of orange or golden berries; their evergreen foliage is useful. Cultivars now on offer are likely to be of kinds proven resistant to fungus diseases.

Rhododendron

Lifetimes are short, one could spend one on the study of rhododendrons without feeling there was much time to spare. By most reckoning there are 600 species, but forms and hybrids abound. In Britain some 2,500 kinds are on offer through nurseries. Many more grow in specialist gardens. They range from species able to make substantial trees to diminutive items that hug the ground and exist just above. Foliar appeal is variable and is much more than a casual acquaintance with popular hybrids and the ubiquitous Iberian species, *R.ponticum,* might suggest. This last is a plant whose introduction may have been a mistake since it has taken over vast areas of the countryside. It has spread because of its wide use as a rootstock; the graft may or may not have lasted. The rootstock certainly would have persisted and, by suckering and seeding, ensured that it further extended its territory.

Rhus glabra: smooth sumach   d   1 to 2m (3 to 6ft)
R. typhina was listed amongst the trees, *R.glabra* is a close relative but is of bushy form and has smooth young leaves and stems. It is a fine foliage plant with well-posed pinnate leaves up to 45cm (18in) long and made of from thirteen to more than double this number of leaflets. These are long spear shapes, each 6 to 12cm (2½ to 4in) long and with margins that may be lightly or more markedly teethed. Tight plumes of flowers similar to *R.typina*'s appear in summer and fade from red to rust with persistent fruitheads. Leaves die off with typical brilliance. There is a deeply cut-leaved form called 'Laciniata' which is attractive. Cut to the ground every second year, the stock will throw up strong growth with leaves like some massive exotic jungle fern.

Ribes
The currents are of the auxiliary brigade, useful, and in season, not without splendour. Some are grown for their foliage, *R.alpinum* 'Aureum' has more or less typical currant leaves, three or five lobed, bright yellow in youth, remaining bright though not so yellow when aged. *R.sanguineum* 'Brocklebankii' is a primrose-leaved version of the flowering currant. The light colour is held the whole season but is best in partial shade where the sun cannot burn the leaves.

Rosa
Healthy foliage of hybrid roses can be almost as attractive as the flowers, but too often this means dedicated spraying to ward off black spot or mildew. High-gloss greens, rich maroons and purples gleam in the sunshine. Many species are in a different league, resistant to disease and often naturally pleasing in leaf form and shrub shape. Small leaves of *R.farrerii* look well, especially on a neat rounded bush with no hybrid gawkiness. Others, like *R.rubrifolia*, have size and colour to commend them. This grows strongly upright with a suckering habit that soon makes a plant 1.5 to 2m (5 to 6ft) high with plenty of arching branches to alleviate any suspicion of gauntness. Stems are red but covered with purple bloom. Five or seven little leaflets to each leaf are neatly teethed and coloured shades of purple-red with a greyish cast.

Others have different appeals. *R.wichuraiana* is vigorous and low growing making good cover for rough banks and other such places. This cover becomes a dense carpet of highly polished, deep-green typical rose leaves. As branches can do a 4m (12ft) sideways leap in a season, this is not a plant for a cramped spot. Come midsummer the green is decorated with posies of snow-white 5cm (2in) flowers, half or a full dozen to each bunch.

Rosa rubrifolia. Rich plum- and burgundy-coloured neat leaves, often with a greyish bloom, are held on dark stems. Single small pink flowers are not very distracting

Dwarf willow, *Salix lanata*,
silvery in youth, grey later.
Males have large upright
golden powder-puff catkins,
females are more discrete
and grey-green

Rubus
Having done battle with well-armed weedy brambles the gardener
is unlikely to be too well disposed to this lot. However there are ex-
ceptions. *R.deliciosus* is without any offensive weapon. Bright-
green leaves are like a blackcurrant's but of lesser calibre. *R.tricolor*
is a favourite vigorous ground-cover plant listed in Chapter 10.

Salix
Shrubby willows are interesting, more interesting than eye catch-
ing, but a few are excellent. Try to get the best forms of any species
you decide to grow. The males have the showier catkins.

S.lanata: woolly willow   d   75cm to 1m (2 to 3ft)
Worth growing either as male or female, it is always a fine foliage
plant but some clones are better than others. Leaves are 2 to 6cm (1
to 2½in) long and 2 to 4cm (1 to 1½in) wide. Buds in spring glisten with filigree silken hairs and as they expand this silken silver is
preserved on both surfaces. Male catkins are large, honey-coloured
domes to start with and then golden as the pollen is freed, female
ones are a modest green. As leaves age they lose the silkiness but
remain silvery or metallic grey. It makes a sturdy or spreading firm
shrub perhaps 1m (3ft) high.

S.repens: creeping willow   d   15 to 40cm (6 to 15in)
It leapfrogs and suckers its way around to form a mass of arching
slender stems with thin willow leaves up to 2cm (¾in) long. The
type is shiny green, but there are more attractive silver-leaved
forms, *S.r.argentea.* It is a scrambler, not for the obsessively tidy gardener.

S.reticulata
A worthy species listed in Chapter 12 for things minuscule.

Santolina chamaecyparissus: Lavender cotton   e   30 to 60cm
                                                                                (1 to 2ft)
As youngsters these are neat, rounded little bushes with unusual
thin leaves that have midribs 3 to 4cm (1 to 1½in) long to which
are stuck a series of short tufts of thick white felt. The stems are
thickly clothed with these long leaves, the whole glistening even on
a dull day. A mass of flowers appears in summer, tight yellow compositae buttons bereft of the ring of outer ray florets. Flowers are
held on slender wiry stems perhaps 15cm (6in) above the main
bush.

S.rosmarinifolia   30 to 60cm (1 to 2ft)
Similar to last but bright green.

Sarcococca
Evergreen shrubs always neat and handsome in leaf and managing
well in shady places. Coming to the fore as gardens shrink. They
enjoy moist soils but have no particular fancies.

S.hookeriana humilis   e   45 to 75cm (1½ to 2ft)
Rather like butcher's broom with lots of upright stems from the
ground; a tidy shrub with lots of narrow oval pointed leaves. These
can be 2 to 8cm (1 to 3in) long but only 1 to 2cm (½ to ¾in) wide.
There is a vein running around each leaf just clear of the margin.
Flowers are white and insignificant very early in spring, more noted
for scent than sight. *S.confusa* is a taller cousin perhaps 1m (3ft)
high, with clear, shiny light-green leaves.

S.hookeriana digvyna   e   60cm to 1m (2 to 4ft)
This form is only half the height of the species and is much tougher.
Narrow shining green leaves and graceful exemplary habit make it
very popular.

S.ruscifolia   e   60cm to 1m (2 to 4ft)
Well mannered with dark polished leaves broader than its relatives.
Tiny flowers can open whilst the red berries from last year's blos-
som are still present.

Senecio x 'Sunshine' (*S.greyi* of gardens)   e   60cm (2ft)
This useful New Zealander has masses of silver and grey foliage,
bushes being much wider than tall. Individual leaves are oval and
measure 5cm (2in) long by 3cm (1¼in) wide. Prune bushes for
tidiness and to promote fresh growth. Backs of leaves are white, top
surfaces are covered with silky down in youth to give them a silver
sheen, but age to colours of baser metals, though light and attractive
at all times. Masses of yellow daisies are a midsummer bonus. Late
summer cuttings root readily. Good shrub to contrast with darker
leaved kinds. Low enough to grow in front of or against these darker
things.

Skimmia japonica   e   1m (3ft)
Both male and female forms are needed to provide the brilliant red
berries that brighten the late autumn, winter, and early spring.
Tough oval leaves look as though they are made of plastic. Leaf
colour is normally a rich deep green but in very limy soils they may
become anaemic and need added peat or a dose of Epsom salts to
counter the lime. One must be careful about the several named
forms. 'Fromanii', as usually offered is a very good female with large
leaves and lots of good-sized berries, but some nurserymen sell a
male under this name. 'Rubella' is a widely available male.
S.reevesiana (S.fortunei) has both male and female flowers on the
same plant. It is low growing with dark narrower leaves; the dark
red, oval berries last for months.

Ulex europaeus 'Flore Pleno'   e   1m (3ft)
This is the double form of the common gorse. Leaves are thin
pointed strips or just spines. Stems are the same green. The overall
effect of the plant is of an intricate, rounded, green mass wider than
tall. It is covered with golden yellow blossom in spring but may produce a few flowers at any time.

Three evergreen viburnums:
*V.tinus, V.rhytidophyllum,
V.davidii*

Vaccinium

These are allied to the ericacea and are lovers of acid peaty soils.
There are evergreen and deciduous members. *V.corymbosum,* the
blueberry, is a neat spreading plant making a mass of erect branching wiry stems with oval pointed leaves 2 to 9cm (1 to 3½in) long.
White or blush-pink heather-type hanging flowers are produced in
May, but it is at its most colourful at the season's end when the
foliage becomes many shades of red before being shed. *V.vitis-
idaea* is our native cowberry, a glossy evergreen with dark red
berries. An improved form, 'Koralle', is stronger and has larger
berries. The shrub, whilst only about 25cm (10in) high at most, will
extend sideways by its running rootstock to make a considerable
dimension. The whole is a dense tidy mass of polished dark green.

Viburnum tinus   e   2 to 3m (6 to 9ft)

Viburnums are good-natured bushes with plenty to contribute to
the garden. *V.tinus,* one of the most widespread of all shrubs, has
hardy, very dense dark foliage cover of clean-cut tough entire leaves
together with posies of white flowers from autumn through to
spring. As buds are pink, it maintains the popular colour pattern of
the family. At present 'Eve Price' is probably the best form with
foliage as good as any and with large, round, flat, tight arrangements
of small five-pointed little white stars accompanied by many rosy
buds. Dark cloud forms of leaves are useful foils for such as the
witch-hazels with yellow or orange tassels on bare winter branches.

V.opulus   d   3 to 4m (9 to 12ft)

The guelder rose of the hedgerow is found in the garden most frequently in the double form commonly called the snowball bush. This double can be impressive with many rounded well-packed cream snowballs in the unseasonable month of June. It naturally foregoes the bunches of shining berries that are such a feature of the wild plant. Foliage could pass for that of a currant or maple with three, four, or five lobes. Fresh mid-green is maintained until it takes on a variety of fiery shades in autumn.

V.x bodnantense   d   3 to 4m (9 to 12ft)

This name covers the hybrid offspring from *V.farrerii* and *V.grandiflorum.* They have become indispensable in keeping winter gloom at bay, producing pink-budded white blossom from autumn through the winter into spring. They inherit all the *V.farrerii (V.fragrans)* hardiness with some of the greater largesse of *V.grandiflorum. V.farrerii* is no mean performer itself with lots of tight, sweet-perfumed posies in the dull months. However the hybrids tend to eclipse it with greater vigour and generosity of bloom. 'Dawn' is the widespread clone. A young plant soon becomes an almost solid thicket of upright and arching brown stems with a multitude of close-clasped pink-budded white flowers. The foliage is excellent, young stems are red and the young leaves are suffused red, a healthy bronze that is not entirely lost through the year. Leaves are impressed with vein networks but are polished and healthy looking. 'Deben' has a more upright and staid form, flowers are almost pure white in larger tight bunches so that it looks good from autumn onwards. Foliage is similar, but perhaps the shrub shape is less satisfying.

V.carlesii   d   1 to 3m (3 to 9ft)

This has a lot going for it. Deeply fragrant blossom in wide-domed clusters 5 to 8cm (2 to 3in) across is pink in bud and vividly white open. The foliage is admirable with broad ovate, healthy-looking rich green leaves. They are paler below and covered with a similar glittery down as the younger stems. Veining is well marked and the margins of leaves serrated in an irregular manner. They die off in bright good order. 'Aurora' is a cultivar with rather more richly coloured flower clusters, nearly red when developing, but rich pink in bud and white open. Flower buds are mounted in autumn in readiness for the spring debut.

V.x burkwoodii   e   1.5 to 3m (4 to 7ft)

This has the deciduous *V.carlesii* as father and the evergreen *V.utile* as mother. It decides to be evergreen with wide-angled grey branches and large, polished, leathery dark-green leaves. A proportion die off each year, a higher proportion in bad winters, and these take on brilliant orange and scarlet tints. Large clusters of sweet-scented five-pointed flowers are tightly arranged posies as wide as 10cm (4in) across. They are blush pink in bud and white when open.

7   *Herbaceous, Bulbous, and Annual Endeavour*

The herbaceous element of garden design will have greater emphasis in one garden than another. Here it may provide the main excitement of the growing year while in the neighbouring garden, shrubs and trees are the centre of attention with herbaceous plants filling awkward spots or maintaining interest until shrubs mature and take over their allotted area.

In the gardener's sense, a herbaceous plant is normally defined as one that has a perennial rootstock, and grows from ground level to go through its annual cycle of leaf, flower, and seed production in one growing season before dying back to the resting rootstock for winter. Most fit these specifications; some, like many hellebores, are more evergreen.

The Bulbs

The first move of the year will be bulbous. Snowdrops push bunches of leaves upwards. Crocuses, daffodils, tulips and many other genera follow suit. A few, like some muscari, will have been in a hurry and produced leaves in the autumn. Most bulbs' leaves are simple working jobs, though the sight of them coming through the soil is exciting, signalling a new year. Some tulips have beautiful foliage. Purple striped *T.greigii* and its hybrids have already been mentioned (p.24). Other species have their own points; *T.linifolia* is one of the prettiest. It makes a rosette of 6 to 10cm ($2\frac{1}{2}$ to 4in) long, narrow grey-green leaves flat on the top of the soil like some unusual starfish. They usually have waved margins, an unusual but decorative lightly crimped style, the very edge of the leaves often being marked with a pencilled line of red. The popular species, *T.tarda,* is another that makes ground-hugging rosettes but in bright polished green with longer leaves.

Size alone makes the leaves of *T.fosteriana* interesting. They can easily measure 20cm (8in) long by half as wide — a generous width. Opulent proportions are inherited by Darwin x fosteriana hybrids marketed as 'Darwin Hybrids'; they have acquired hybrid vigour along the way, but whilst the species keeps its largest leaves quite low the hybrids dispose theirs in the standard manner of the old Darwins. Leaf size is impressive with smooth curving grey-green surfaces.

Later other bulbs can create dramatic foliage. The upright stems of *Lilium martagon* have whorls of foliage at widely separated intervals, each whorl of entire leaflets arranged like the spokes of a wheel with the stem as the axle. It has style. Most American species follow suit. The sight of a good clump of *L.pardalinum giganteum* is a delight. You can stand and watch the strong stems growing, not

one deviating a half a degree from the vertical, rich green leaves being more highly polished than *L.martagon's*.

Rhizomatous plants come into quick spring growth before the heat and drought of summer, and before other plants crowd them out. Lily-of-the-valley is an example; spikes pierce the soil with uniform vigour, they unfurl in beautiful unison, each identical leaf blade shining fresh lively green.

Further along the border another perfect ballet sequence is enacted by Solomon's seal, *Polygonatum multiflorum*. Stems shoot up in spring with neatly arranged alternate leaves closely clasped. These are long spear-shaped bright pea-green ones, entire, and noticeably longitudinally veined and somewhat arching. Stems reach up to as much as 80cm (2½ft) describing a gentle arc to allow slender ivory white bells to hang. Leaves remain pristine until they fade to autumn fawn. Other species are as decorative. *P.x hybridum,* from *P.multiflorum* x *P.odoratum,* is able to grow over 1m (3ft). It seems to burst with health as soon as it appears above ground. Shooting up rapidly, the last third of each turns to the horizontal so that bells are well displayed. Another species, the very narrow-leaved *P.verticillatum,* can reach 1.3m (4ft) with whorls of very narrow lanceolate leaves. Bunches of small, greenish-white bells are held close to the stem below each of the leaf whorls.

Making a dead set for honours in the foliage stakes come the dicentras. *D.spectabilis,* is best known, spectacular in flower and as splendid in leaf; it is certainly worth growing for the lovely foliage

Phormium tenax variegatum is the New Zealand flax, now found in many coloured forms, all with strong long leaves half way between a large grass and a yucca. The dark-leaved *Helleborus foetidus* (front) grows wild in Europe, including Britain, whilst *Rodgersia podophylla* comes from Japan

alone. Flowers in rich pink and white hang along wide-arching stems above the foliage at a height of perhaps 60cm (2ft). These flowers have given rise to many fanciful names, such as 'Dutchman's breeches', 'bleeding heart', and 'lady in the bath' (to see the lady you turn the flower upside down; I think you would search in vain for a Dutchman with trousers that would make you think of dicentras; of bleeding hearts I have no knowledge). Plants grow energetically, succulent shoots unfurling well divided long-stalked leaves that make clean-cut patterns in space. It is half way to being a fern, but retains a succulent feel. Smaller is the glaucous blue-green leaved *D.eximia* which grows some 40cm (15in) high but spreads much wider. Flowers are a dark ruby red, best in the form 'Adrian Bloom', but really this is primarily a foliage plant making a good stab at imitating a fern with wide triangular fronds divided into an airy double pinnate pattern. There is a white-flowered form in commerce which is only half the height ('Alba').

The Herbaceous

The huge daisy family is not one immediately associated with foliar beauty; flowers after all are the main thing, but there are daisies that have pleasing leaves. Some of the pyrethrums are examples. These hybrids of *Chrysanthemum coccineum* were once grown in considerable quantities for the cut-flower market. All the named hybrids and seedlings make mounds of rich green, much-cut ferny leaves which remain fresh and attractive after the flowers have gone.

A telling contrast between the dark spurge *Euphorbia amygdaloides* 'Rubra' and the sparkling *Pulmonaria saccharata* 'Argentea' (White Windows)

Some of the leaves of the handsome hardy genus *Geranium*

Senecio cineraria 'White Diamond' the whitest of all this handsome species. It is best cut back in spring to encourage fresh strong growth and inhibit some of the small yellow daises. Below is the cut-leaved grey-green foliage of the sulphur-yellow flowered *Achillea* 'Moonshine'

Some achilleas have interesting leaves. The tall flat-headed 'Gold Plate' has bright green neatly and intricately cut soft ferny foliage. The more easily managed 'Moonshine', standing only a third as high at 50cm (20in) with sulphur-yellow flowers, has rather similar ferny foliage but this time in grey and silver.

Many plants grown for flowers are well supported by their foliage. Hardy geraniums are well endowed with character leaves freely produced so that a mound of interesting shapes is present from early spring till nearly winter. The dwarfer form of *G. sanguineum*, *G. s. lancastrense*, is a spreading plant with lots of five- or seven-lobed leaves cut right back to give a palmate effect but with each lobe further divided. Pinky-mauve flowers are freely produced, the plants standing approximately 30cm (1ft) high. *G. endressii* has many round rosy pink flowers and three- or five-lobed leaves that are boldly serrated. Hybrid 'Russell Prichard' has rich-coloured leaves particularly deeply lobed.

Hosts of Hostas

Spring and summer are the most important seasons for the hostas. True they last well until the first severe frost arrives, but the greatest enjoyment lies in watching the clumps begin to grow in spring, new leaves unfurling and then growing to full summer potential.

The once-despised hosta now has its own society. The number of cultivars is already legion and is increasing all the time. Breeding of new types is being extensively undertaken in America, in Britain,

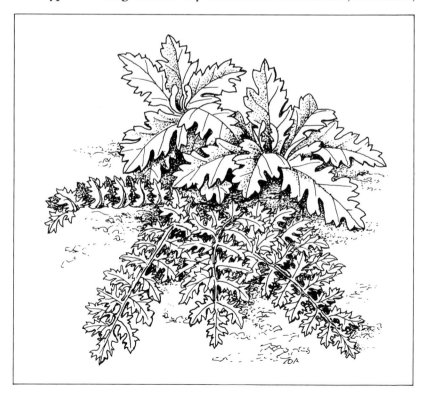

and elsewhere, meaning that gardeners are taking more note of leaves. Not that some hostas have no floral charm, but possibly more than ninety per cent of a hosta's appeal is in the leaves.

There is diversity. The colour palette is wide. Form varies within the rather strict design specifications of the genus. Size is measured from the minute to the hugely opulent.

Some degree of order has been brought to the botany of the genus by a number of distinguished gardener/botanists, a duality of interests that must never be taken for granted. In Britain more than a hundred types are on sale but many more are being grown and exchanged by enthusiasts. Take care buying hostas. View the plants first as, whilst botanists and specialists may have arrived at broad agreement on nomenclature, some nurserymen may not be up to date with their labelling. Some sympathy can be spared for the trade; an old favourite is renamed so the commercial grower must decide whether to relabel or wait until next week when another botanist may decide to restore the original name.

H. sieboldiana is one of the most impressive large-leaved species. A fine form is *H.s.* 'Elegans' *(H.glauca)* with each blue-green leaf up to 30cm (1ft) long and a surprising 22cm (9in) wide. Broad blades are decoratively marked with veining. The blue-green remains cool and fresh until the frosts turn the leaves to pale gold before they collapse. Flower stems mark the spot through the winter like the weathered masts of a sunken windjammer.

H. fortunei 'Albopicta' is one of the many variegated kinds, most lovely in late spring and early summer when its broad leaves are clearly marked with many tones and shades of green and yellow, a delicate-painted patchwork pattern that fades later. 'Aurea' is as strong but its huge leaves are a pale shining lemon or lime shade, most effective in a dark spot or beside some soberly dressed plants. 'Marginata Alba' with cream-edged leaves is another strong worthwhile plant. Most surprising can be 'Picta' with broad pointed leaves nine-tenths a pale cream, with only the margins somewhat irregularly picked out in green and with sometimes just an odd splash of one- or two-toned green midleaf. A clump is almost surrealistic.

'Thomas Hogg' is another very effective strong kind with large pointed leaves of rich green but broadly margined in white, one of the whitest edged of the lot. A clump or two of this makes a fine contrast to one of the plain-coloured ones like *H. sieboldiana* 'Elegans'.

It is difficult to have too many hostas in the garden, they fill in odd corners or contrast with totally different foliage. They can be a feature just by themselves. Broad, bold, low-lying leaves in an interesting clump or clumps may be just the thing to emphasise the delicate filigree work of ferns, of fennel, or thalictrums. They may be just as telling a contrast with shrub foliage and in greens, yellow, and whites look effective against a whole gamut of shrubs, some straightforward greens but also purpled cotinus or silvery senecios. They grow well in most soils; they enjoy moisture without wanting to stand in a stagnant bog. They are stunning by poolside or stream, but are as impressive in light woodland, often most telling when

several clumps are grown in association but with space between. There are few plants with greater root masses. Lift and divide clumps every few years and cast aside the older portions — a good young 'un beats a good old one.

OPPOSITE
Another striking hosta combination: the bright-leaved *Hosta fortunei* 'Albopicta' with a richly coloured cultivar *H.*'Halcyon'

Summer

Summers are often a complete fiction, an amalgam of nine parts anticipation to one part disappointment. However, plants seem to enjoy it. Unpromising little bits that saw the winter through are now splendid high achievers. In one spot is a classical plant, a clump of black-green lacquered, large-leaved acanthus. Its flower spikes in purple, silver, and green are unusual but the leaves are the real feature.

There are a few species and several forms. *Acanthus mollis* is a large-leaved dark one with each leaf being up to 60cm (2ft) long and half as wide. Margins lack the spines of some kinds, but they are heavily indented. Plenty of leaves make a rounded mound of rich colouring with a height of maybe over 1m (3ft) when in bloom with white or pale lilac-pink flowers. This is usually offered as 'Latifolius', a form larger and stronger than the type.

Widely grown *A.spinosus* is best given space to colonise. Once planted, it is able to look after itself with impressive masses of arching large leaves. These are a polished dark green, heavily cut back to the midrib so that each leaf is almost a series of long, wickedly pointed leaflets which are themselves lobed and teethed. From the summer till autumn it is rarely without some of the 1 to 1.5m (3 to 5ft) flower stems with purple-hooded paler flowers each protected by a spine. The type is very impressive, but *A.s.spinosissimus* forms have dark leaves made more splendid by the leaf spine and main veins being strongly etched out in silver.

You may plant acanthus in the assurance that it will be there to stay; it is at least as permanent as a shrub. Should you decide, in the fullness of time, to move it, you could be in for a man-sized job. The thick fleshy roots delve down deeply and, if broken fractions are left in the original site, they will probably grow upwards and produce fresh leaves the following season. They are impressive, they are tenacious of life, do well in poor soils, and are able to withstand prolonged droughts.

Through spring into summer, the herbaceous plants begin to move. From beneath a few dried-up rusty leaves clumps of *Alchemilla mollis* get into early action. Rounded leaves grow as an opened fan from the leaf stalk, the main veins marking off segments of the fan, but this is not completely flat, and this means that they often look their freshest and most decorative after rain when water droplets nestle like jewels, one set in the centre of almost every leaf where the fan veins meet. To fresh light green is added the frothy lime-yellow blossom of a mass of little flowers, useful for the flower arranger but a reminder to remove the flowering stems later or seedlings will appear everywhere. Alchemillas cope well with very dry conditions and thrive anywhere. Some euphorbias, sedums,

The frothy mustard-coloured flowers are much used by flower arrangers, but the rounded lobed leaves of *Alchemilla mollis* are a constant source of delight, especially after rain when each leaf holds in its centre a sparkling water globule better than any jewel

Herbaceous plants; *Anemone hybrida, Geum chiloensis* 'Mrs Bradshaw', and *Potentilla*

geums, and geraniums are also drought resisters.

Moist spots attract some splendid plants that signal their affinity to water by glowing good health. Here is a wide mat of gold, leaves of the yellow-leaved mutant of the meadowsweet of roadside ditches and wet grassland. The type is a wayside weed, pleasant but a weed nevertheless. Pinnate foliage of our mutant, *Filipendula ulmaria* 'Aurea', is neatly serrated and makes uniform golden cover about 20cm (8in) high. Whilst not so ready with flowers as the type it does attempt to bloom, something to deprecate as its talents are foliar not floral. Cut the stems away and enjoy the leaves.

More tailored are the astilbes, well known for their love of water. The size and general well-being of the deep-green divided leaves, pinnate and not unlike one of the bolder smaller ferns, depend in part on the amount they have to drink. Plume-like flowerheads come in shades of red, pink, and white. Some of the darker-flowered forms are likely to have somewhat bronzed glistening foliage. Taller and with more prolific divided pinnate leaves is *Aruncus sylvester (A.dioicus)* which, grown in moist soils, can reach over head high with divided plumes of tiny cream flowers. This frothy mass appears perhaps in June and, fancifully, could be thought to have been constructed from a thousand creamy pipe cleaners with their free ends pointing in all directions. The flowers are over quickly but the foliage is a healthy dark, lustrous green and is attractive from early spring until the end of the summer.

It surprises me to find in the very dry shallow soils of our garden how well the distinctive *Ligularia przewalskii (Senecio przewalskii)* has grown. In former gardens clumps in moist areas had done well. Polished, dark mahogany stems are almost black, leaf stalks are as dark and the under-surfaces of the large leaves are a polished deep maroon. The upper surfaces are well held and are a basic pointed heart shape, somewhat more rounded in the cultivar 'The Rocket', but the margins are imaginatively cut in a series of bold incurves and are left saw-edged. The effect is splendid. A series of twisty yellow flowers are stuck onto the top of the flower stems to make decorative slender spikes 1.6 to 2.3m (5 to 7ft) high. We grow 'The Rocket' clone more than others because it is as stylish as any and the flowers are rather brighter.

Strength and beauty are generously combined in *Macleaya cordata (M.cordifolia),* one of the most majestic of foliage plants. It is full of vigour but stately with it. A new plant, with a single stem its first season, will produce many runners just below the soil surface so that the next year may see several dozen stems. As each can be 1.6 to 2.6m (5 to 8ft) high it means that space must be allocated for the plant to show its potential. It all sounds terribly invasive, but the plant is well worth growing if you have a spot that can take its height. The stems are strong upright canes grey-green or flushed warm beige.

The well-stalked bold leaves are like no others, basically rounded or heart-shaped as the names *cordata* and *cordifolia* mean. Well-marked veins help emphasise the palmate lobed form. The palmate effect is achieved with some deeply rounded indentations but both these, and the lobes themselves, are rounded not pointed. The bold lobes are divided with lesser curved indentations. Lobes to the sides are often left with two fingers while the terminal lobe may be scalloped into a five-fingered design. The colour is a palish, pleasing green, suffused with pinky bronze. Plenty of these leaves are prominently displayed from soil level to head height, and so, as well as being grown towards the centre or back of a bed or border, it can be brought forward either in an isolated round bed with little else, or as sudden confrontational clumps by a pathway or a prominent summertime spot. Atop are multitudes of tiny pinky-fawn flowers. The hazy colouring above is pleasing, the foliage is stylish and magnificent. *M. microcarpa* is similar, perhaps coming into bloom a little earlier.

The thalictrums are a family with obvious beauty of foliage, some are less well endowed florally. *T. flavum,* the yellow meadow-rue, is a colonising plant with a root stock that is a seething mass of yellow stoloniferous underground stems. In spring they send up stems 60cm to 1m (2 to 3ft) high, the leaves much divided into little leaflets either entire or three lobed, and looking like a loosely arranged maidenhair fern but more blue-grey in colour. The quoted height is achieved by the May and June flowering stems that carry a flock of tiny yellow flowers like gnats dancing in the air giving the effect of a yellowish haze above the more important leaves. It is a good foliage plant but must be planted where its colonising proc-

Blue-grey firm foliage of stylish *Thalictrum flavum glaucum,* a strong plant of non-invasive habit

livities are permissible.

T. flavum glaucum has an altogether more circumspect character, is sturdier and more beefy. It is slow to extend its territory but it is an excellent foliage plant. The stems grow strongly to 1 to 2m (3 to 6ft) and plenty of leaves are produced, firmer and larger than those of *T. flavum*. It is arranged in the same maidenhead-fern manner, with a lot of leaflets to a leaf, each leaflet being often as broad or broader than long, and possibly up to 2cm (nearly 1in) wide. The colour effect is of a steely blue, somewhat more green in older age. A piece taken from the plant might at first glance be thought very similar to an aquilegia. The flowers are of little consequence. Whilst strong, it is wise to support the tall stems to save them being brought low by a storm just when they are at their most effective.

The species *T. delavayi* to which *T. dipterocarpum* is now referred has both leaf and flower appeal. The leaves are again arranged pinnately with each leaflet held well clear of its neighbour on thread-thin stems. These leaflets are of a basic heart shape but with three lobes. They are a fresh, slightly glaucous green, the pose is light and airy. Flowers appear in the summer months of July, August,

Macleaya cordata with its unusually shaped foliage, actually grey-green above and near-white below *(Author)*

and September with lots of loose panicles of bright pink chubby blossoms, normally four petalled with conspicuous yellow-anthered stamens. The plant can grow to 70cm to 1.3m (2 to 4ft), but the fine 'Hewitt's Double' is more compact at little over half the height.

The similarity to aquilegia foliage is acknowledged in *T.aquilegifolium,* a robust tall species with leaves doubly or trebly pinnate. Glaucous blue-green leaflets, each have three to six lobes and measure up to 4cm (1½in) across. Flowers are fluffy with stamens, but purplish from the petals. Petals are really sepals, like those of all this genus. 'Thundercloud' ('Purple Cloud') is a particularly good form in bloom from late spring into summer standing around 1m (3ft).

Thalictrums remain in good order from the unfurling of the first leaflet until autumn collapse.

The Herbs
A glance at an old herbal will show many plants listed for their real or supposed utilitarian virtues. Here be cures for all manner of ills, flavourings to make dull or tainted food more palatable, scents to

The brightness of lemon balm *Melissa officinalis* 'Aurea' is a perfect foil to *Geranium* 'Johnson's Blue' and an aquilegia *(Author)*

combat evil smells of less hygenically concerned times, aids to digestion, and help for restful sleep or for procreation. Any plant bereft of all other beneficence was assumed to have aphrodisiacal powers.

Some are bold things. Lovage can be majestic, growing with great abandon with many divided pointed shining leaves not dissimilar to those of celery, but larger and vastly more prolific. Flowering stems, some 2 to 2.6m (6 to 8ft) tall, create wide lime-yellow umbelliferous heads. This determined perennial plant is well worth culling to give bite to a green salad or to make a fine soup. Angelica is similarly umbelliferous but is biennial. Seedlings make a loose rosette of clean-cut pinnate glossy leaves; the second season sees the flowering stem furnished with fine celery foliage and topped with impressive wide round-domed heads of lime-coloured flowers. Seed heads bear huge quantities of flat disc seeds. It is a plant of architectural value. You may candy the stems, or, according to Culpepper and others, employ it 'for all epidemical diseases caused by Saturn.' Just the thing to have close at hand, and it is still used nowadays to 'briefly ease and disperse all windiness and inward swellings.'

Smaller plants are decorative and make worthwhile contributions to the herb garden, or may be integrated into the garden proper. Balm has been grown for many uses from classical times onwards. We employ it as an extremely useful bright plant in its yellow-leaved form, *Melissa officinalis* 'Aurea'. Bits are torn from an established plant and planted between dark-leaved plants and shrubs to provide light in the darkness. Heart-shaped, serrated leaves form an initial rosette in early spring, and from this expands a cheerful mound 20 to 30cm (8 to 12in) high and wider. Above all are lesser leaved flowering stems. Flowers are unspectacular. Veinnetted leaves dispense their bright gold and, if one is plucked, it gives also a lemon scent.

Few can rival the vivid velvety rich green of tansy, *Tanacetum vulgare,* in full growth. Rounded low mounds of intricately divided pinnate leaves are a joy. The tight heads of yellow button compositae flowers are not indecorous, but many will prefer the foliage. Few have such a velvety plush look and feel, though the crushed-leaf odour is acrid rather than bewitching.

Mints, thymes, and sages, all have points of foliar beauty and bless the nostril. Sages are often grown for looks alone, embossed greygreen oval shaped leaves making a low sub-shrubby mass, but far more effective in a coloured form. Episcopal pigment suffuses the leaves of *Salvia officinalis* 'Purpurascens', and there is also at least one variegated form of the purple kind with irregular splashes of creamy white. Even more colourful is *S.o.* 'Tricolor' with the basic grey-green augmented by veining and splashes of pale yellow and pinky-mauve. A compact yellow-leaved form is sometimes available and there is a widely grown kind with golden variegation. They can make an interesting collection but are best in their younger stages. As pieces root easily it is no hardship to keep all young and healthy looking.

Purple sage *Salvia officinalis* 'Purpurascens', the golden variegated *S.o.* 'Icterina', and small-leaved *Thymus* 'Golden King'

A few plants of fennel, *Foeniculum vulgare,* can be used with great effect in many places to give a quiet touch to a particular spot. The filigree foliage of this herb, the leaves reduced to the thinnest of rich-green threads, can be a complete contrast with normal foliage around about. There are various forms, the commonest being purple, which are just as worth growing. The plants will rise to anything between 1m (3ft) and 1.6m (5ft). They will persist for a few years, but it is wise to have new stock coming on. More of the fine foliage can be encouraged by cutting back the flowering stems before they reach too high.

The Silver-leaved

At different times a plant may look sparkling silver or plain grey. Some of the brightest summer plants become a bedraggled grey in winter. In most cases a covering of fine hairs produces the light-splitting silvery effect; when these wear off, or are coalesced by continual rain or frost, the silver becomes base pewter. However, we would be poorer without a good smattering of these lighter coloured leaves, especially in the lush high summer. Even such an ordinary thing as 'lamb's tongue' or 'donkeys' ears', *Stachys byzantina,* is valuable for its thick carpet of heavily felted long oval leaves that shine brightly through the summer months. It is useful in difficult dry spots or for interplanting between shrubs to give a light foil. The ordinary type will send up tall-stemmed carmine-pink flowers, messy and graceless to behold. The alternatives are to

Leathery large-leaved evergreen *Bergenia cordifolia*, with *Crocosmia masonorum* like a large montbretia, creeping *Cotoneaster dammerii*, and *Stachys byzantina* (better known by the unflattering names 'lamb's lugs' or 'donkey's ears')

remove the offending parts, or more judiciously to plant the form 'Silver Carpet' that sublimates all flowering propensity into leaf production.

Often the production of hairs or scales is a mechanism to help leaves withstand dry weather, minimising the effect of transpiration. The silver plants are likely to come from warmer, drier climes and this indicates their possible station in the garden. They need plenty of light and plenty of good drainage. This applies to many of the silvery artemisias and helichrysums. They range from small rock garden species to others several feet tall and impressive in the border. The common *Artemisia absinthium,* wormwood, with much divided ferny foliage, is made silver white with a thick layer of felt. It can grow to 50cm to 1m (18in to 3ft) high with a mound of leaves doubly or trebly pinnate, each up to 9cm (3½in) long and two-thirds as wide. The yellow-flowering heads give it extra height but these are not really worth the effort. 'Lambrook Silver' is a good, widely grown cultivar.

The fleshy leaves of *Sedum spectabile* are grey-green and glaucous. They look impressive as they build up their height with regularly arranged rows of thick leaves. The wide heads of pink flowers stand 40 to 50cm (15 to 18in) high and look good as rust-brown winter seedheads. *S.s.* 'Autumn Joy' can be 70cm (2ft) high with the widest heads of the species, starting silvery pink but becoming more orange and then rust. Leaves are thick and silvery. *S.rhodiola (S.roseum)* is less tall and forms wide masses of gleaming blue-green glaucous foliage arranged on many stems from the central base. Each stem has its many fleshy rounded leaves neatly arranged more or less at right angles to the stem and in a very even systematic style. It glistens throughout the winter as well as in the growing months, new growth overcoming the old in the spring.

Euphorbia myrsinites is not dissimilar to the last-named sedum. It stays close to the ground and has a number of white stems furnished with thick oval leaves that are silver blue. Each stem is topped in spring with typical spurge flowers of wide-whorled bracts of sulphur lemon. *E. characias wulfenii* can make a clump some 1 to 1.3m (3 to 4ft) high, as permanent and impressive as many a shrub. The many long stems are well furnished with oblong leaves in an amalgam of blue, grey, and green. Huge rounded flowerheads add mustard and lime colours to silver and grey.

Thistles of the right kinds are attractive. Some are giants like the biennial *Onopordum salterii* that can grow to a massive 3m (9ft) or more. Snow-white stems branch and are as bright as the much-cut silvery leaves. It has large blue flower heads. On a smaller scale are some of the eryngiums with green and silver leaves. *E. bourgatii* has spiky much-divided thistle-like shining ones of silvery green with dark stems that reach perhaps 60cm (2ft) with good-sized tight cones of silvery-blue flowers. Around the base of each cone is a wide collar of heavily armed spikes, metallic in appearance and highly decorative. *E. variifolium* has broad, more rounded, less heavily armed leaves in mounds over the ground. They are green, marbled

Euphorbia characias 'Wulfenii' with the feathery grey of Artemesia absinthium, and a flowering broom to the left (Author)

silver. Branched stems arise above the leaves to 80cm (2½ft) and carry blue flowers in tight bosses below each of which radiate very long slender silver spikes perhaps six or seven from each flower head.

Some, like *E.amethystinum,* vary the pattern; this species by having low-down, much-cut pointed foliage of shining green. Stems reach 30 to 60cm (1 to 2ft) high, but the upper part of the stem with its foliage, the smallish knobs of flowers, and their surrounding ring of six to eight teethed spikes are all coloured vivid shades of rich silvery-blue.

'Miss Willmott's Ghost' is the name given to the monocarpic *E.giganteum;* it dies after flowering. It honours an interesting and successful gardening personality. Initial basal leaves are tough, rich green, heart-shaped ones; they make a ring from which a flowering stem arises in the second season. The stem, and the sharply teethed stem-clasped leaves, together with the large flower heads, all glitter in bright silver. This is an outstanding garden plant, the flowerhead and stem leaves being most intricately and surely worked; the very wide, much-armed collar of bracts below the cone of flowers is as dazzling as the most finished of ornamental silver metal work. The head produces shoals of seed so that this monocarpic plant may be grown knowing the next generation is always there ready to carry on.

Evergreen spurges: the greyish soft-green *Euphorbia characias wulfenii*, the rich green *E.amygdaloides robbiae* (centre), and silvery fleshy *E.myrsinites*

Winter

Winter arrives and much of yesterday's foliage has vanished. Some plants soldier on. The euphorbias are particularly in evidence. Some have been mentioned already. Others like *Euphorbia amyg-*

daloides, in many forms, remains fully dressed and stands the winter well. The type is a rich green, long-leaved species growing to 30cm (1ft) or more and making a shrub-like mass. Often the leaves are suffused with reddish purple. There is a distinguished form, *E.a.rubra,* with leaves enriched with wine colours. *E.a.robbiae,* for long maintained as a species in its own right, makes a rounded mass of lacquered dark-green leaves that look healthy and are neatly disposed around the stems.

Sedums, sempervivums and such like hardy small things survive the worst of winter. For other plants, now is the season to begin the serious matter of flowering and seed production. Hellebores take their turn; the Christmas rose, *H.niger,* with tough, dark foliage will try to protect its large white flowers from the worst of the winter, and is first to defy the weather and open its flowers. Others follow till the last of the Lenten roses, the Orientalis hybrids, have faded.

The most notable foliage species is the prodigy formerly known as *Helleborus corsicus,* which we are learning to address as *H.argutifolius.* Good plants are almost shrubs with stems rising in an arching manner to about 40 to 50cm (15 to 18in) and ending in a cornucopia of apple-green buds and open bowl-shaped flowers. Leaves of the toughest of materials are honed to the finest of polished finishes, each leaf being composed of three leaflets strikingly serrated with sharp points. Leaf blades are a rich green ornamented with palely traced venation. The terminal leaflet is a basic spear shape, the side ones are more fully extended and rounded on the far

Most useful of arums for foliage effects, *Arum italicum* produces its fresh leaves in the autumn and holds them through the winter

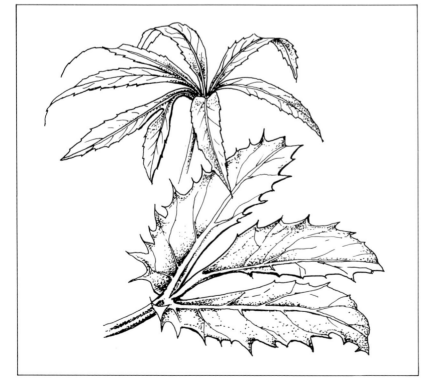

Winter-flowering evergreens *Helleborus foetidus* with black/green palmate leaves and *H.argutifolius* with polished handsomely toothed mid-green leaves

side of the prominent midrib. The under-leaf surfaces are paler. Stems are a pale green. The whole makes a most interesting sculpture. Flowers fade and seed pods spill their harvest, the stems die away, but before this happens new growths will emerge from the central rootstock all shiny and pristine with the promise of abundant new life. New growth can be touched with mahogany or red.

The native *Helleborus foetidus* has dark-green leaves, each arranged like a palm of seven to eleven narrow leaflets. It has the merit of being completely evergreen and making plants up to 70cm (2ft) high that look shrub-like. Black-green foliage is distinctive, especially next to a pale plant or against light stonework.

A Shortlist of Outstanding Herbaceous Foliage Plants!

Acanthus spinosus spinosissimus
Dicentra spectabilis
Eryngium giganteum
Helleborus argutifolius
Hosta sieboldiana 'Elegans'
Hosta fortunei 'Albopicta'
Macleaya cordifolia
Polygonatum multiflorum
Thalictrum flavum glaucum

The handsome evergreen herbaceous *Helleborus argutifolius*, formerly *H.corsicus* (Author)

8

Grasses, Bamboos and Ferns

Grass as a lawn forms a huge proportion of many gardens, maybe too large, but this is not part of the present brief. There are other considerations; decorative grasses range from small tufts that may snuggle into the rock garden to giant clumps of pampas-grasses. Similar to some grasses in appearance are New Zealand flaxes though these belong to the Lily natural order. Our choice is widened by an influx of these *Phormiums,* plants of undoubted theatrical beauty but of varying degrees of hardiness.

Grasses are neglected as garden plants, which is a pity as their huge diversity of form, size, colour, and habit can provide interest and beauty not only in the growing months but in some cases in winter. Some are adapted for particular habitats. Shade and woodland are no good for our lawn species, but the native woodrushes *(Luzulas),* and kinds like *Milium effusum* with its golden variant, 'Bowles' Golden Grass', delight in such a spot. In damp areas and sometimes even in water a series of sedges and rushes look especially effective. The zebra rush, *Scirpus tabernaemontanii zebrinus* (*Schoenoplectus t.z.*) is going to tempt many with its bands of

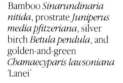

Bamboo *Sinarundinaria nitida*, prostrate *Juniperus media pfitzeriana*, silver birch *Betula pendula*, and golden-and-green *Chamaecyparis lawsoniana* 'Lanei'

yellow and green as surely painted as the black and white poles supporting road beacons. Many tiddlers are suited to the rock garden or can join the miniature world of the sink or trough. There are plenty for all sites; in beds and borders they may be planted like shrubs, often looking best when different types are planted in association to make one realise afresh how very different they can be.

The Bamboos
Of course the bamboos are grasses, ranging from small species only about 30cm (1ft) high to those that can reach 7m (20ft) or more. They are distinct from more usual herbaceous grasses by their reinforced woody parts and unusual lifecycle.

Whilst most grasses flower annually, some bamboos may not bloom for several decades. After blooming the canes bearing flowers die. The belief that all the plants of a species will die simultaneously is incorrect. Vegetative divisions of a single plant may all produce flowers at the same time and these canes die. Rarely does a complete clump die, though it can look sick for a while. New growth will eventually be mustered and the cycle be restarted.

Most bamboos belong to three families; *Arundinaria, Phyllostachys,* and *Sasa.* Their main characteristics are as follows:

Arundinaria
Upright round canes with ill-defined internodal grooves. Cane sheaths are persistent. Branching starts at the cane top before beginning lower down. Active rootstocks may be colonising.

Phyllostachys
Thicker canes, somewhat zigzagging, internodes marked by flattening alternately and grooving. Branching starts at the bottom of the canes. Sheaths perish. Rootstock forms clumps.

Sasa
Has dwarf plants. Leaves are larger than other bamboos, margins die off brown in winter. Branches, usually one, but unusually in pairs. Sheaths are persistent. Rootstock energetically colonising.

Of the arundinarias, *A.japonica* is very hardy and in cultivation makes 3 to 4m (9 to 12ft) high clumps. It may have a place in the wild garden but is not as attractive as some other species for important spots. It may be identified by the under-surfaces of the leaves being of two colours, about one-third grass green and two-thirds metallic grey. *A. murielae* is more pleasing. Brightly coloured in leaf, it has green sheaths, and grows slenderly upwards, then forms a pattern of graceful arching stems with little thin leaves. If only one bamboo is to be planted, this could well be the choice. A tight elegant clump 3.5 to 4m (10 to 14ft) high, it grows with ease in almost any site.

Variegated bamboos can be very striking. There is a good white one, *A.variegata,* and an even more striking golden one, *A.viridis-*

OPPOSITE
Arundinaria vagans is one of
a number of easy dwarf
bamboos. This one rarely
gets above 1m (3ft) high but
in the open it can be invasive,
so it is best in a container
(Author)

triata. A. variegata grows 1.3m (4 to 5ft) with leaves 20cm (8in) by 2.5cm (1in) boldly coloured a deep green and shining white on the upper surfaces, below it is less surely differentiated. *A. viridistriata* can be taller at 2m (6ft) and needs to be grown in full sun to encourage the rich golden variegation of the broader leaves. Upper leaf surfaces are vividly striped green and gold, usually more gold than green. Well grown it is one of the brightest of all variegated plants, but in shade the colour is lost. One or two dwarf forms of this golden kind grow only some 30cm (1ft) high.

For a specimen clump you could choose *A. murielae,* or one of the *Phyllostachys, P. aurea* or *P. nigra. P. aurea* is very robust, making clumps 3 to 5m (10 to 14ft) high. Perhaps your umbrella shank is made from it, you will know it from the swollen part of the cane below each node. Young stiff canes are shining green, but become yellow with age. Bold upright stance, golden canes, and narrowly cut leaves make a fine sentinel clump.

P. nigra starts out with young olive-coloured canes, but the second year these become mottled purple black, and in their third season they adopt their permanent black. Canes are topped with abundant foliage from slender branches, the weight of foliage en-

New Zealand flaxes with their handsome, sword-shaped leaves, *Phormium tenox* 'Maori Sunrise' being in the foreground *(Overbecks)*

couraging graceful arching towards ground level. The grace of the clumps is as obvious as the black cane colour, which is best developed in full sunlight.

All the bamboos are atmospheric plants with something of the mysterious Orient about them. In the smaller garden, perhaps none manifests this feeling more than the Sasa species. *S. tessellata* is a star performer. It grows up to only 1m (3ft) although the canes may reach double this dimension. They are bowed low by the weight of the many huge leaves 60cm (2ft) long by 10cm (4in) wide. Leaves hang to one side of the cane when reaching for the light and look all the more luxuriant so displayed. The gardener will want to emphasise the lush foliage by placing it close by small-leaved kinds, be they bamboos or not. Given plenty of moisture and food a plant will grow and spread strongly. *S. veitchii* is even stronger growing and when conditions suit it, the colonising can be invasive. Leaves are almost as large, their rich green contrasted by the pale margins which, although green when young, soon lose their chlorophyll to give a variegated effect.

The Bolder Grasses

Unless you become addicted to grasses and the garden is taken over, you may be content with a few bold kinds and a number of somewhat smaller ones to use in beds and borders. They represent a neglected sector of gardening. The exception is the pampas-green, too well known to need description or commendation. However several distinct forms could be used to greater effect including a few dwarf ones. *Cortaderia selloana* 'Bertinii' grows only 75cm to 1m (2 to 3ft) in bloom. 'Pumila' reaches 1.2m (4ft) and is very free of flower. Very distinctive is *C.s.* 'Gold Band' *(C.s. aureo-lineata),* which makes a widely arching tumbling mass of leaves that are boldly margined, rich golden yellow but become all over a warm orange-old gold with age. It grows to about two-thirds the size of the type and is very free flowering.

The ease with which pampas-grass can be propagated and the fact that it is so well known tends to eclipse the claims of other similar-sized plants, some of which are less heavy. One of the finest of these is New Zealander *Chionchloa conspicua,* a strong evergreen making clumps 2 to 3m (6 to 9ft) high, but clearly more open, graceful, and finished in leaf, habit, and bloom. Light green, very narrow leaves have an orange midrib. It starts to flower early, perhaps in late spring and can be so decorated until late summer.

Grown as isolated specimens, both *Miscanthus sacchariflorus* and *M. sinensis* are large architectural clump-forming grasses. The first may reach an impressive 2.5m (8ft) pressing strongly with the arching leaf blades 1m (3ft) long and 2.5cm (1in) wide. They are a yellowish green with white midribs, but they become orange in autumn and remain colourful through the winter until the early spring cut. Flowerheads are silky white or mauve-tinted very divided arrangements hauled into prominence in late summer. *M. sinensis* grows to 2m (6ft) in Britain with blue-green leaves and comes into bloom as late as mid- or late summer with wide heads some 30cm (1ft) long. These remain through the winter. There are a number of very showy variegated forms of this species, *M.s.variegatus (M.s.foliis stiatus)* is a notable plant with a wide central cream line and silver-striped leaf blades. *M.s.zebrinus* is like the type but someone has gone around and painted horizontal patches of pale yellow on all the leaves.

For bright light golden masses, it takes a lot to beat the performance of *Glyceria maxima* 'Variegata'. This grows rapidly to make a spreading mass of arching leaves 50 to 75cm (1½ to 2½ft) high each 5cm (2in) broad and very boldly striped with white or creamy yellow. Young growth is flushed mauvey-pink and in old age, before leaves fade for winter, turns purple. Vivid mid-year colouring is so dramatic that it will need handling with care or it will dominate all surrounding characters. It can be grown in the border, by water, or even in water.

Large grasses are best grown like specimen shrubs, but the kinds that are up to a metre high can be incorporated into borders and beds with other plants, herbaceous or shrubby, and can make a distinctive contribution, either integrated with these or as a colony of contrasting grass type.

Of the golden-striped grasses, *Alopecurus pratensis* 'Aureovariegatus' is splendid, probably outdoing all others. It makes a steadily increasing-sized plant with foliage up to about 30cm (1ft) but capable of more. The leaf blades are striped paleish green but are broadly margined in deep gold; these gold margins join to form solid gold leaf tips. It is best cut back to stop it flowering and the resulting growth always looks brighter and forms denser cover. It is useful towards the front of any bed or border.

Another bright-leaved plant is *Milium effusum* 'Aureum' ('Bowles' Golden Grass') which makes a rounded plant of arching leaves 30cm (1ft) long and 1.6cm (¾in) wide. It comes into growth early and keeps its even gold through the year. It is particularly good in light shade where it can illuminate surrounding growth. A single plant looks well, but a lot planted to make an informal carpet is very pleasing indeed.

Molinia caerulea 'Variegata' is an attractive, strongly tufted grass with leaves 30 to 45cm (12 to 18in) long growing up and arching over to make a light-green plant some 30 to 40cm (12 to 15in) high. The colouring is a slightly bluish-green with a prominent creamy-yellow central stripe. It grows best on neutral or acid soils.

A fine twelve-month grass is *Deschampsia caespitosa* which makes dense tufts of very narrow rich-green leaves. These can be 60cm (2ft) long but only a tiny .5cm (⅕in) wide. It is evergreen and makes a mound of about 30 to 45cm (12 to 18in). It has dainty light flowerheads each up to 55cm (nearly 2ft) long and 20cm (8in) wide. It is best in moist semi-shaded places but you may find it in the countryside in open spots.

There are several blue grasses and *Helictotrichon sempervirens* is a fine one. Large tussocks are made of many arching blue-green

OPPOSITE
The purple sage *Salvia officinalis* 'Purpurascens' with spiky grass *Helictotrichon sempervirens* and friends *(White Windows, Wilts)*

narrow leaves 30cm (1ft) long. The flowering is of many tall, light, gracefully drooping heads that starting blue-green become fawn.

Judged by flowers, a leading contender amongst perennials is *Stipa calamagrostis*. With dense tufts of narrow dark-green leaves 30cm (1ft) long that curve over to make a neat base, they produce loose widespread summer heads of light feathery flowers. These flowering stems remain attractive until the end of the winter. The relative *S.pennata* is most distinctive in bloom. The leaves are bright green and nearly twice the length of the first species. They bend over to make a charming tuft. Flowerheads are made of a number of gracefully arching and pendant narrow feathers, the flower head itself being as much as 30cm (1ft) long.

Small Grasses
There are huge numbers of these smaller grasses that can look well in the rock garden or in the front of beds. One of the most popular is *Festuca caesia* which could probably win the prize as the bluest of all plants were there such a competition. It makes a very thick-tufted mass of narrow stiff upward-pointing leaves of blue. Look around and try to find the bluest clone offered. Once you have your

Strongly growing variegated pampas grass *Cortaderia selloana* 'Gold Band' framed against a dark hedge, with *Yucca filamentosa* and flowering red hot poker, *Kniphofia (RHS Wisley)*

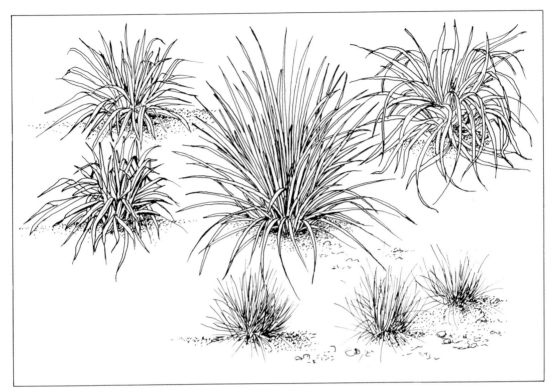

Grasses *Molinia caerula* 'Variegata', gold and green pattern (top right); *Helictotrichon sempervirens (Avena candida)* with narrow-leaved hummocks of blue-green about 45cm (18in) high (centre); *Hakonechloa macra* 'Albo-aurea', a charming Japanese grass growing only about 25cm (9-10in) and bright lemon and gold from early spring till winter (left, two tufts); and *Festuca glauca*, the very popular bluest of grasses making neat hedgehog tufts only 15-20cm (6-8in) high lasting all year round (below)

plant it may be divided every two years and given a severe hair cut in early spring and the summer to encourage the new growth that has the brightest colour.

The golden variegated form of *Hakonechloa macra, H.m.* 'Aureola', is a dense, arching mass of narrow leaves in shining golden yellow with the odd green streak emphasising the colour. It is very bright from early on until the leaves die. It is especially good in light shade and needs propagating by division as it does not come true from seed.

The sedges are almost all tidy bright spiky characters. Some are tiny; *Carex firma variegata* can be grown in a trough garden being only 5 to 10cm (2 to 4in) high with 2.5cm (1in) long spiky leaves. The leaves are boldly margined cream yellow. Larger, but still small, is *C.morrowii* 'Aurea Variegata', a plant that makes a dense ever-green mound of 30cm (1ft) long leaves, made brilliant with a broad central golden stripe. There is a scarce tiny variation that has leaves only about 8cm (3in) long and curled like an unusual starfish.

Hardy Ferns

As already mentioned in Chapter 4, the Victorians were very in-terested in ferns and collections of many kinds were built up. That there are some 50 wild species of fern in the relatively small area of Britain is surprising, but this forms only a tiny proportion of the worldwide population of between 10,000 and 11,000 species in 240 families. Many of these belong to the tropical rain forests and

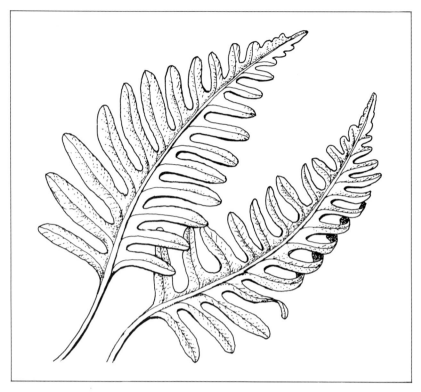

Common Polypody
(Polypodium vulgare) can
creep over the bole and
trunks of mossy trees or grow
on mossy banks and walls. Its
evergreen fronds will
decorate shady spots where
there is little soil or obvious
nourishment

are not hardy outside in Britain. However there are many from America, New Zealand and other places that are happy in our climate.

Given clean air, ferns are very undemanding plants. They coped with life on this planet for millions of years before the first flowering plant evolved. Their roots like well-aerated soils with good drainage. Some enjoy lime, others prefer slightly acid conditions, many are indifferent. The hardy kinds divide into the deciduous and the evergreen, although this division is not all that clear-cut as there are some that retain green fronds until spring, provided that the winter weather does not become overpoweringly fearsome, in which case they die back.

The terms used in describing ferns can be a little daunting but some precision is needed to differentiate between many superficially similar kinds. The rootstock may be tufted like the common male and lady ferns, or a creeping one like bracken. The extent to which the rootstock creeps or branches is very variable. The stem of a frond may be an insignificant length in proportion to that of the leafy blade, but can be as long as or longer than the leaf blade. The midrib of the leafy part is called the *rachis.* The leaf blade may be one entire piece like that of the hart's tongue. If it should be lobed it is called *pinnatifid.* If the frond is divided down to the rachis like an ash leaf it is described as *pinnate.* If each of these leaflets or pinnae are then lobed the fronds are classed as *bipinnatifid,* if they are divided into fresh small leaflets or *pinnules,* they are *bipinnate.* If

these tiny parts are then further lobed we arrive as *tripinnatifid,* and if they are cut to form fresh little pinnules the frond is *tripinnate.* And so on.

A useful diagnostic feature of ferns in the wild is the colour and shape of the fruiting bodies on the fertile fronds. These are the *sori* which release spores when ripe. Ferns do not have seed. The spores that germinate in suitable spots produce a completely different plant, a green flat disc from which arise male and female organs. Sperm released from the male parts disperses through a film of water and the lucky ones unite with egg cells to start a small sporeling, the beginning of what we recognise as the fern plant proper.

Now having done our homework, let us consider what kinds to grow:

Osmunda regalis: royal fern

We start with royalty. This is the largest of British ferns, capable of a magnificent 3m (9ft) but more likely to be half this stature, and still mightily impressive with the blades of the sterile fronds 30cm to 1m (1 to 3ft) long and 30cm (1ft) or more wide. These are bipinnate and form a wide arching mass with, in the centre, the upright fertile

OPPOSITE
Very bright grass *Hakonechloa macra variegata* 'Aureola' with *Hosta undulata* 'Albo-marginata', and ferns including the hart's tongue *Asplenium scolopendrium* (foreground) and the large royal fern *Osmunda regalis* (background). By the water's edge is the skunk cabbage *Symplocarpus foetidus (RHS Wisley)*

The largest of British ferns *Osmunda regalis*, the royal fern, which grows all over Europe, Asia, North and South America, as well as in Africa. Here it is seen in spring with its crosiers unfurling *(Author)*

fronds quite distinct in the rusty-brown tight heads that have given rise to the name 'flowering fern' though of course there are no fern flowers. These fronds have been likened to the flowering heads of astilbes.

This is a large deciduous plant suited only to a position that can take a bold design stroke. It loves water and needs a damp site. Even the huddle of rusted remains in the winter is not without its decorative effect.

Athyrium filix-femina: lady fern

This is one of the commoner British ferns and is called the lady fern recognising that it is lighter and more graceful than the similar-sized male fern. It has tufted rootstocks that produce fronds 20cm to 70cm (8in to 2ft +) in length and 7 to 25cm (3 to 10in) wide. It is to be found in hedgerows, ditches, or moist woodland and this is probably the place to enjoy it. Some 300 named varieties were once available for the garden. All those now on sale are easy, hardy, deciduous plants looking most lovely in the spring as they unfurl, and they remain fresh through the summer into the autumn. *A.f.-f.* corymbiferum are varieties that are so crested that they have layers of pleated tassels along the edges of the fronds and at the ends. As a frond may be 30cm (1ft) to over three times this length, the whole plant can become a wonderful intricate design. Particularly good forms of *A.f.- f. corymbiferum* are marked out by having the name of the finder or raiser tacked on.

Athyrium filix-femina plumosum is the name given to a series of shining, light-green creations that look as if the first puff of wind would blow them away. The fronds will be at least tripinnate and are more likely to be cut four times. They are rather smaller than the type and are best grown in a sheltered spot where they are not going to be battered too much by the wind. The leaves are like the finest lace.

Dryopteris filix-mas: male fern

Some of the best cultivars of the male fern are somewhat more expansive than the raw standard species. *D.f.-m. decomposita* has noticeably more finely drawn fronds whose gracefulness is enhanced by being more widely spread than the erect type.

Dryopteris pseudo-mas cristata: the king fern (*D. borrerii cristata* 'The King')

It is certainly a regal character with fronds 30cm to 1m (1 to 3ft) long and coloured a bright golden green, noticeably more yellow than neighbouring types, and these fronds are very neatly crested the length of the margins. The fronds are displayed more uprightly than some but the tips are attractively arched outwards.

Dryopteris dilatata: broad buckler fern

Comparing a frond of this with one of the typical male or lady fern shows just how much the extra division of the frond adds to the intricacy and beauty of the whole. The male and lady ferns are basically bipinnate, the broad buckler fern may have bipinnate parts but the main growth is tripinnate and this makes the wide, bright green, triangular fronds all that more interesting and worthy of garden space. It can grow a frond up to 90 by 40cm (36 by 15in) and stand up 1m (3ft) high. With several such flat fronds pointing outwards a plant can look most imposing. It enjoys a moist spot.

OVERLEAF
Dryopteris filix-mas 'Grandiceps', a form of the variable, very robust and widespread male fern *(Author)*

Polystichum aculeatum: hard shield fern

This robust kind in dark polished green is capable of fronds measuring 1m (3ft) long. A plant can be easily approaching 2m (6ft) across and so needs placing where it has space. The newly purchased young specimen in a 10cm (3in) pot looks very sweet but gives no hint of its growth potential. There are a limited number of varieties and the most prized of these is the miracle rejoicing under the name *Polystichum aculeatum* 'Pulcherrimum Gracillimum'. You will need a longer label. This prodigy has pinules so slender as to be threadlike. Each frond ends with very finely divided tassels. It is as hardy as the type and well-grown mature specimens can be a miracle of ferny creation.

Polystichum setiferum: soft shield fern

This is lighter in colour and texture than the last, with a velvet rather than a leather or metallic finish. The type is well worth growing in its own right, but it is mother and father to a huge family of choice kinds. Nearly four hundred of these were honoured with names in Victorian times. Most were lost following the two world wars and changing economic times. We now have relatively few of the named cultivars, but they are amongst the most pleasing of British ferns. *P.s.* 'Acutilobum' has narrow fronds and pinnules and these are more pointed. The fronds arch widely and carry numbers of bulbils along the rachis at the base of the pinnae. 'Acutilobum-divisilobum' is distinct in being a lot more finely drawn, the ultimate divisions being very narrow indeed. Bulbils are also produced, but not so freely.

Asplenium scolopendrium: hart's tongue (*Phyllitis scolopendrium*)

This fern is likely to be found growing wild in most parts of the country in damp shaded spots. In the wetter parts of the country it may grow freely along hedges, ditches, or can almost clothe a woodland floor, but in drier parts it will look to wet ditches, the sides of wells, and such like moist cool microclimates to set up home.

We can invite the wild plant into the garden because it is always pleasing with its shining, unbroken long tongues in vivid green. Alternatively we may be happy to enjoy it in the wild and bring some of its variants into the garden. A good form of *P.s. crispum* could be one of the best. It grows as easily as the type, and has the same long, unbroken fronds glistening richly, but it has a major sartorial deviation — a goffering iron has been used the length of the margins to

produce an effect like that of an Elizabethan ruff. Plants of this and other variants are valuable for being stubbornly evergreen. *A.s.cristatum* ignores the dress rules of the type; its fronds divide many times and each division ends with a widespread crest. It sounds as though this would spoil the design of the type and be messy, in fact it creates an interesting and pleasing sculpture.

Matteuccia struthiopteris: shuttlecock or ostrich fern
The botanists have had a field day with this plant giving it many names, and I expect it will have more in the future. However the gardener briefly curses the botanist and calls it by its common name. All other ferns mentioned in this chapter are British natives, this one is a foreigner but it is hardy and grows wild here, introduced into the wild with the connivance of fern-fanciers.

Thin black creeping rhizomes that run just below the soil surface enable this fern to expand its territory and in the spring each end develops a fresh green fountain of a plant. It is deciduous. The new fronds unfurl in the spring to make a likeness to a shuttlecock perhaps 45cm to 1.5m (18in to 4½ft) high. One marvels when looking down the shuttlecock funnel at the precision with which these sterile fronds link together. The fertile ones may appear later in the centre as dwarf, stout, brittle-looking grouped growths of a metallic rusty- or chocolate-brown. A plant soon becomes a colony.

Small Ferns
Whilst the larger ferns are plants of hedgerow, ditches, and woodland, a few small species live in the mortar of old walls. These are pretty little things and can be grown in the garden either on such walls, in the rock garden, in miniature trough gardens, or even in pots. Not all foliage effects have to be large scale — examining these little things can engender just as much admiration and awe. These are our easiest native dwarfs.

Immaculate little maidenhead spleenwort *Asplenium trichomanes* that grows on walls and makes a fine evergreen rock-garden plant

Asplenium trichomanes: maidenhair spleenwort
The young fronds lie flat against the rocky wall usually in a vertical spot rather than atop the wall. As new fronds appear they unfurl over previous ones, eventually building up into a mound. Each narrow frond can be from 5 to 30cm (2 to 10in) long with perhaps thirty to forty pairs of flat pinnae, each of which is rarely more than 4mm (¼in) across. The green of the fronds contrasts with the dark, almost black, threadlike rachis along which they are threaded. It loves life in a wall or rock crevice where the drainage is perfect. The name maidenhair spleenwort would suggest a likeness to maidenhair ferns but this is a misconception.

Asplenium ceterach (Ceterach officinarum): rustyback fern
This is another dwarf fern to be found growing happily in the mortar of old walls. It can stand far more drought than most ferns. Its fronds are tough, thick, leathery pinnatifid ones, silky silver as they unfurl, but yellowish green on their mature upper surfaces and a rich rust-

coloured felt below. Fronds are 5 to 20cm (2 to 8in) long and usually not more than 2cm (³⁄₄in) wide.

Asplenium ruta-muraria: wall-rue
This very dark green little fern grows in walls with limey mortar. It probably does better there than in other sites that might be tried in the garden. It is distinct from the last two, especially by having stalks to the fronds that are as long as the blade, or more likely up to double that length. The pinnae are more or less ovate and may be borne in threes like a tiny clover leaf, perhaps four such groups being held in each frond. The plants make a rounded growth on a vertical wall often where one would have thought it impossible to sustain life.

Increasing Your Ferns
It is a cardinal sin to collect ferns from the wild, there are too many of us and too few of them. However, all is not lost as the propagation of ferns is not all that difficult and is full of interest.

Division may appear to be the obvious way to increase a fern but this is not all that easy with many. Of those mentioned the best for dividing are the lady ferns, the male ferns, and hart's tongue. The best time is in early spring just before new fronds unfurl. The more root that can be kept with the divided plant the sooner it will establish itself. The divided plants should be tucked in firmly, but with the soil open for the roots to explore. Old dead roots, rootstock, and fronds can be cut neatly away. Do not bury the plant more than a fraction deeper than it was previously growing.

The shuttlecock fern produces so many new plants from its wandering runners that the problem is likely to be to find homes for them all. Too many plants crowded and jostling together tend to detract from the perfect symmetry of each. It is therefore good policy to thin them out and make more friends by giving away the surplus.

The evergreen little rusty-back fern *Asplenium ceterach* grows on walls. Its long roots enable it to withstand periods of considerable drought. Rain will resurrect an apparently completely desiccated plant

The shield ferns are easily propagated from the many bulbils they produce along the midrib of each frond. A frond can be pegged to the ground and, by working some open compost around the bulbils, these will be encouraged to root and soon form independent plants. Alternatively a frond may be detached and laid in a tray of compost rich in grit and leaf mould. Weighed down on this moist compost the bulbils soon root if kept in a cool, shaded frame or greenhouse.

Vegetative propagation ensures like producing like. The natural method of increase by spores will allow the species to increase correctly with chances of some variation within specific limits. Special forms may, or may not, reproduce by spores. Some are sterile, and others will give a wide variation in their offspring.

One may tell whether the spores are ripe by taking a small piece of fruiting frond and placing it on a piece of clean white paper overnight in a warm spot. Normally after twenty-four hours ripe fruiting sori will have released far more spores than needed onto the paper. If you are in a particular hurry, hold a piece of fruiting frond over

paper and place near a source of gentle heat (a lit light bulb). Then watch to see if dust-like spores are released onto the paper.

Spores should be sown thinly on a sterilised surfaced in as aseptic conditions as possible. The container should be clean, the compost, of leaf mould and grit or crushed mortar, sterile. A pot of compost may be rendered sterile by pouring boiling water over it until it is all thoroughly wet and heated. When it is nearly cold the spores may be very lightly dusted over the surface from the tip of a knife or spatula. Whilst the compost is cooling, and after sowing, the containers should be kept completely covered to prevent unwanted freelance spores of mosses and other things finding a home. The sown pots can be kept warm, and after some weeks a greening of the surface should mean that all is going well. The containers need to be kept moist by taking up water from below. The male and female parts will appear over the green cover and fertilisation will take place and tiny plantlets begin to grow. These can be removed once they are big enough to handle and be grown on in similar compost. They must not be allowed to dry out.

The rearing and growing of ferns is one of the most satisfying aspects of gardening, and there is always a chance of raising a particularly good form that will make you the envy of other fern enthusiasts.

OPPOSITE
The sensitive fern, *Onoclea sensibilis* in happy combination with the bold palmate leaves of *Rodgersia aesculifolia*, and hostas *(Savill Gardens)*

9 *Wet, Water and Waterside*

Nowhere in the garden does foliage take on more dramatic roles than in and by water, or where the ground oozes with wetness. The big drinkers, adapted to such sites, show off their good health in glowing, often large, leaves and stems.

The plants that are now for consideration can be arbitrarily divided into three: those that live in the water like water lilies; those that grow beside water with their toes possibly well into the water like many rushes or water-loving irises; and those that may eventually flounder if their rootstocks are permanently submerged but do not mind periodic immersion and, whilst enjoying copious draughts of water, expect some drainage around their bases.

The water itself is a main design element. Pools, of whatever size, reflect their surrounds and the sky, and thus can create different atmospheres as the surrounds and the weather changes. Where water is incorporated in the plans, it needs to belong in the whole, be it a natural or formal effect. A raw-edged pool or stream offends. However, plants grow so quickly that such an offence is likely to be short lived. The danger may well be the opposite one, that the water-loving plants thrive so energetically that they almost obliterate the water. We need to plant discreetly.

The three categories of water-loving plants will be reviewed under the headings: moisture lovers; marginal plants; water plants.

Moisture Lovers

Many of the plants listed here could grow well enough under normal garden conditions, but they take on that extra gloss where there is abundant moisture. The hostas will manage extra width and length. Narrow-leaved irises, like *I. chrysographes* and *L. laevigata,* will form thick, upright clumps, grass-green in the growing months and rusty-brown through the winter. The rodgersias are another clan that anyone can grow, but which are so much more impressive in moist situations.

The rodgersias are a small genus of similar plants grown primarily for their foliage. Perhaps the most striking is *R. aesculifolia* and few plants can so vary their height and size according to their diet. They can grow and look fine well under 60cm (2ft), but with plenty to drink in a sheltered position the leaves may be twice as high and with the flowering stems reach 2m (6ft). Leaf design makes a comparison to the horse chestnut obligatory if rather obvious. The leaves are borne on long stalks and held more or less horizontally. Each is composed of perhaps seven leaflets some 12cm (5in) to 30cm (1ft) long and altogether can be up to 50cm (20in) across. Individually these are shaped like those of the horse chestnut, being narrow in the lower part and steadily widening out towards the end. Apart from the very attractive shape of these leaves, they are distinguished by their shiny gloss, their embossed network of veins and the good colour. The healthy rich green is usually suffused by a warm bronze red. The flowers are creamy white, a lot of tiny ones in clusters on stems that clear the leaf level. The clusters are spread along the flowering spikes and are an added element to the midsummer design, but one of far lesser impact than the foliage itself. It is a leading foliage plant. The leaves give themselves enough room to make the most of their size and bold form, plants grow by strong, surface-creeping rhizomes. It does not take long to establish a worthwhile colony.

R.pinnata is similar, just a little smaller and with from five to nine leaflets arranged palmately and a little more pointed than the last. A good stand of leaves 30cm (1ft) or more across and of leaflets normally 15 to 20cm (5 to 8in) long is soon established in the late spring. As with all the rodgersias, a bad late frost can cut back the young unfurling leaves and cause a check whilst the strong plants rally their resources and if necessary produce a fresh crop of leaves. It is obviously best not to plant in a position known to be particularly vulnerable to frost or to high wind which can damage the large leaves when fully expanded. The palmate arrangement is bold and pleasing, the colour is a rich green but can be more or less dominated by a reddish purple. The form *R.p.* 'Superba' is one of the richest coloured leaves and has rather more showy flowers. These are well-branched panicles, spread as a long pointed spike of rosy red blossom with touches of white. They look well in the early half of the summer.

The third species *R.podophylla* growing to 1 to 1.3m (4 to 4ft) is a plant of much the same basic design. Usually each leaf has five large leaflets about 15 to 30cm (6 to 10in) long and 7 to 12cm (3 to 5in) wide. These leaflets are perhaps even more distinctive than those of the other species; they, too, have a rich green colouring overlaid with a reddish bronze cast, they have their network of veins deeply and decoratively impressed, they shine with glossy health, but their form is distinct. Each leaflet is three lobed, and may have two or four lesser-pointed lobes. They grow from a narrow base to their greatest width two-thirds along their length. Apart from the lobing, the leaf margin is also neatly and sharply serrated. Positioned next to plants such as water-loving irises or shrubs with plain flat leaves, the form of the leaves and their intricate detail is thrown into greater relief. The flowers of this species are creamy-white plumes.

For a long time another plant was listed as *Rodgersia tabularis,* but this distinct kind is now known as *Astilboides tabularis.* The generic name suggests the likeness of the white flowerheads to those of astilbes. There are no other points of similarity. The plants need a moist spot without wind. They grow to 1m (3ft) and have umbrellas for leaves. These can measure from a modest 30cm (1ft) to a fantastic 1m (3ft) across. The size of the leaves may leave one spellbound and close examination of the details does not weaken one's admiration. The colour is a light yellowish-green so that they show up well in even a dark spot; the margins of the umbrellas are pleasantly lobed and serrated. Few things can look so impressive as a healthy colony of this plant growing in a moist, sheltered spot. The shelter is important as it is the size together with an immaculate condition that make the plant special — leaves damaged by wind will look horribly ravaged.

Rhubarb sounds unromantic, the botanical *Rheum* is scarcely any better, but *R. palmatum,* in one of its several forms, can put on a very worthy show, especially where its thick roots can channel plenty of water to the large leaves. These are far classier than the utilitarian rhubarb's floppy efforts. They are held on firm stems and are tough textured. Their spreading palmate design is emphasised by the embossed main veins and the sharp points of the leaf margins. As the leaves may be up to 30 to 60cm (1 to 3ft) across, a plant with several leaves looks attractively self-important. The most popular forms are those showing the greatest amount of crimson-purple suffusion through the basic green. 'Atrosanguineum' leads the field and might be termed the 'poor man's gunnera', if that did not sound too dismissive a title. Not everyone has room for gunneras, we can all manage a rheum.

No other plant found at the waterside or in a moist spot can begin to rival the gunneras. Sheer size is the dominant characteristic, but happily this is not to the exclusion of other important features. They are plants of good design, strongly drawn and boldly executed. If space allows, one or more plants should be tried, either of the same or of differing species.

All gunneras will impress. The largest leaved, *G.manicata*, has stoutly stemmed, massive tough leaves perhaps 1.3 to 2.5m (4 to 8ft) across. The basic shape of the leaf is widely heart or kidney shaped, but this outline is lost in the boldly lobed, roughly toothed margin. Everything is on the large scale. The leaf stalks, much armed with prickles, can be like branches 1.3 to 2.6m (4 to 8ft) long. The resting rootstock will build up to be like a crouching animal, as big as a tiger. The flowering parts appear in the centre and are pineapple-shaped, rusty-coloured, many-flowered arrangements.

G.chilensis (*G.tinctoria*) is another huge kind, with leaves 1.3 to 1.6m (4 to 5ft) across on stalks 1 to 2m (3 to 6ft) long. Flower masses are somewhat less long than those of *G.manicata.* Both species are normally perfectly hardy, but it is wise to protect young plants by covering the crown with plenty of bracken, straw or leaves for the winter. Often the plant's dead leaves are used to drape over the crowns. This certainly helps in the colder winters and in cooler parts of the country; British winters are less clement than those of their native Chile and Brazil.

In the moist soils near open water some ferns can look splendid. There is a sense of timelessness about ferns that has a natural affinity for water with its feeling of elemental mystery. The most obvious waterside fern would be Britain's largest, the royal fern, *Osmunda regalis.* It can form wide-reaching patterns of foliage over 3m (9ft) or more across and capable of being as high, although 2m (6ft) is more normal. It is deciduous but winter clumps of brown dessication are still colourful; in spring it is a joy to watch the curled downy young fronds unwind themselves and attain their majestic stature. In summer they are magnificent, but they are attractive in autumn as they turn warm shades of brown.

Where such regal opulence might create awkward pressures on space, it would be prudent to plant instead *Dryopteris dilatata*, the wild broad buckler fern. It has the advantage of being evergreen. Its fine wide fronds are 30 to 150cm (1 to 5ft) long, the blade being a triangle up to 90cm (3ft) by 40cm (16in) in a tripinnate design. These are held in shining green good order until spring unleashes the new flush of growth.

It is in the variety and contrast of leaf types that wet or boggy sites can score so heavily. The many moisture-loving primulas, grown primarily for their flowers, are not without leaf appeal. The candelabra primulas, like *P.japonica*, create wide healthy rosettes of crinkled, light green, long oval leaves spread over the ground. *P.florindae*, with flowers like giant cowslips, has less prostrate, more rounded leaves. Much smaller is water-loving *P.rosea*, whose resting winter rootstocks come into rapid action in spring with vivid carmine-rose flowers and attractive, almost circular leaves.

Other moisture lovers have been mentioned elsewhere; the astilbes cannot be overpraised with their glistening dark fern-like foliage. The golden-leaved form of the meadowsweet, *Filipendula ulmaria* 'Aurea' will provide lighter colour. The stems of red and olive-yellow dogwoods shine in the winter, but are still pleasant in the summer, whilst the variegated *Cornus alba* 'Spaethii' is a flashing pattern of gold and green in the leafy months.

Other plants have not been mentioned. Trollius species and hybrids are lovely in bloom with rounded globe flowers in pale lemon and richer yellow shades, but their foliage, showing their buttercup affinities as much as the flowers, is bright, fresh green and much divided to give a light airy effect. The one that grows wild in parts of our countryside, *T.europaeus,* is as pleasing as any, with pale sulphur flowers. There are brighter forms and larger ones, like *T.* 'Superbus', and all are as attractive in leaf as flower. The hybrids are usually bolder colours with heavier leaves, but can be used with effect when one is not striving for the completely natural feel. 'Orange Princess' can look a trifle upstage.

The marsh marigold, *Caltha palustris,* will grow strongly in moist soils and can be as effective a marginal plant in the garden as it is in the wild. Its healthy rounded leaves and burnished, scintillating, rich golden large buttercup flowers can lean over the water and augment their beauty by reflection. The doubled form is just as easy a plant and has plenty of more persistent flowers. These are built up of many layers of tidily arranged petals. The mounds of the rounded leaves are pleasing enough without the gold.

Nearby, another moisture lover, not entirely dormant in the winter, comes sprinting into action in the spring, its accomplishment in spread, in leaf, and in flower, being in almost exact proportion to the amount of moisture available for its thirsty roots to drink. The monkey musk, *Mimulus luteus,* has healthy, regularly serrated ovate leaves and outreaching succulent stems. The golden flowered are likely to be bright green leaved, the dark red and mahogany ones may have leaves suffused with bronze shades.

Marginal Plants

These can be the most important of water-loving plants because they will be sited at the boundary between terra firma and the new element, water. Except when cascading down rocks, or being artificially thrown into the air by fountains, water is horizontal in feeling. At the margin of the water and in the shallower reaches, plant life may be dominated by the vertical. Water irises thrust swords towards the sky, reedmaces, sedges, and rushes scarcely lean a degree from the true vertical and all look wonderfully effective.

The iris family is one of the most diverse; some members are desert plants, others, like our native species, will grow only where there is an abundance of water. Both British species are fairly large plants, the yellow-flowered *I.pseudacorus* being attractive in flower and with tall, upright, bright flat leaves. The clone 'Golden Queen' outdoes the type in number and size of flowers. *Iris foetidissima* has almost insignificant violet flowers and quite lush fans of long upright leaves. At a maximum length of about 60cm (2ft) these are likely to be shorter than most of those of the yellow flag iris. This species is attractive in late autumn and early winter with seedpods that split open to show vivid orange bead-like seeds. There are effective

ABOVE
*Astilboides tabularis
(Rodgersia tabularis)*, one of
the most impressive of
foliage plants for moist soils.
Leaves turn fawn and warm
brown before late autumn
collapse *(Author)*

RIGHT
Effective strong contrasts of
planes and colour tones at
Knightshayes, Devon – lawns,
hedges and pool with
waterlilies and irises *(Author)*

variegated forms of each, *I.pseudacorus* 'Variegata' is striped green and yellow, extraordinarily noticeable in the spring. There needs to be space for these species and, if space is no problem, another bold stroke might be the planting of the strongly upright species *I.ochroleuca* with long, narrow, green swords topped with flowers of white splashed in the centre with gold.

Other irises are more showy in leaf and flower. *Iris kaempferii* is a miracle in bloom. It will grow well at the margin of water or with the rootstock submerged. Vigorous narrow foliage makes tidy upright clumps above which, from early until midsummer, are displayed magnificent wide blooms with ample petals horizontally spread and with small upright standards. The colour may be white, through many delicate shades to mauves, lavenders and blues, and to burgundy and royal velvety purple shades. The widespread petals of the flowers look almost independent of the relatively modestly sized leaves.

Iris sibirica makes modestly sized but healthy, upright, thick stands of grassy leaves. Its bright blue or purple flowers are not so large as those of the Japanese *I.kaempferii,* but they are still attractive with broad rounded petals worked with golden tracery towards the rear.

An early spring splash of colour comes from the large golden spathes of *Lysichiton americanum,* sometimes called the American skunk cabbage although this common name is more properly used for *Symplocarpus foetidus.* After the 15cm (6in) long spathes have gone, the strong-growing silvery-green leaves get into the action, growing 30 to 90cm (1 to 2½ft) long, the light glittering on the lacquered surfaces and showing up the very prominent pale midrib to each leaf. It is a bold, almost vulgar, plant more suited to the larger landscape. Like so many waterside plants, it looks best in bold plantings, preferably with two or three patches separated by space or lesser-sized plants.

Lysichiton camtschatcense comes later in the spring with plenty of creamy-white spathes, each whorled around their strong poker-like green spike. They are rather smaller, but have similar shining, healthy leaves conspicuously pointed and held by stems that could be mistaken for rounded sheaths. *Symplocarpus foetidus,* the true skunk cabbage, sounds repulsive, but the smell is not dominant. Its huge cordate leaves are 30 to 60cm (1 to 2ft) long and look as tough as old boots, thick textured and heavily veined. It is an arum relative with greenish spathes striped and splashed with purple and lemony yellow. This bold-leaved plant suits the bog or waterside spot where the large shiny leaves can be displayed. It is a plant for the wilder spot.

From rawboned beauties we move to conspicuously stylised plants that can grace more formal settings. The arrowheads, the *Sagittaria,* are an interesting lot of some thirty odd species. The common one, *S.sagittifolia,* is a native plant with pointed bright green leaves of the typical arrowhead shape held on firm upright stems so that the arrow is some inches from the leaf stalk and the two trailing narrowly pointed, backward-pointing lobes of the leaf are some inches to the rear of the stalk. The early leaves will be in the water, later ones are held boldly in the air, and make a distinctive picture, augmented in early summer with light wide sprays of white flowers. In the garden it will be the double form that most will want to plant. This is a fine foliage plant, well worth its place for its 5 to 20cm (2 to 8in) long leaves, but if there are flowers one might as well have the showier and the double is certainly that, the white flowers are now transmuted into a series of little powder puffs.

The reed maces, with their dark pokerheads often incorrectly called bulrushes, can be dramatic in wild watery places; many gardeners are tempted to try to emulate this wild picture within the restricted frame of the garden, but it can only work where there are acres of ground and water. Some foreign species are less rumbustious, *Typha laxmanii (T. stenophylla)* grows to 1m (3ft) so that it is not insignificant although two-thirds or a half the height possible by the native species. More slender in its narrow upright foliage only .6cm (¼in) wide, the male flowers at the tip of the flowering stem are formed as a 4cm (1½in) long bottle brush, the female part is some 10cm (4in) lower and is a showy, rounded, rusty red, 14cm (5in) long and an impressive 10cm (4in) wide.

Altogether the daintiest, and perhaps most bewitching of reed maces, is *T. minima.* This can be planted in small pools without fear of it taking over. It is a slender graceful plant making a maximum height of 75cm (30in) but it could be half this height with clumps of the most slender of leaves perfectly erect. A leaf will only be .2cm (¹/₁₀in) wide. Flowering stems are tipped by 4cm (1½in) of the male flowers directly above the 5cm (2in) of the dark chocolate female ones which make a rounded ball somewhat more of the rugger shape than that of Association rules.

The true bulrush is *Scirpus lacustris,* which, with its very narrow leaves and stems, can grow to imposing heights, 2 to 3m (6 to 9ft). The unusual form, *S. albescens,* is the one likely to be planted. It is a strong plant and a contrast to its neighbours. Half the height of the type, it is without its invasive propensity. Stems and the few meagre leaves are white with only a few broken green lines randomly distributed. There is a tendency for the rhizomes to revert to the full green and these must be cut away before they dominate the whole.

A very popular bulrush is the striped *S. tabernaemontani* 'Zebrinus'. In rich soil, growing in water, in a position of full sun, this plant will produce a lot of narrow, severely upright, leafless stems banded horizontally white and dark green. The height depends on age, soil, and climate. Stems may be expected to reach 45cm (18in) but can reach over 1.5 (5ft). It is deservedly one of the most popular of all plants for pools, especially those of modest proportions.

Water Plants
The water lilies are of so many types a book could easily be written about them. They range from tiny ones that grow in pools no deeper than 15cm (6in) and which will be happy with a maximum spread

of 30cm (1ft), to those that will colonise huge tracts of water and can cope with depths of a metre or more. The pattern of rounded leaves on the water surface has that touch of magic that almost invites one to step on as onto a stepping stone. If they become too crowded the leaves can be forced into the upper air, which is not so attractive. One needs water around the leaves for the perfect picture.

Aponogeton distachyos, the water hawthorn, makes a pattern of oval-oblong, rich-green leaves spotted and stippled with purple floating on the water often in a circle. Leaves can be 15 to 20cm (6 to 8in) long and are likely to be accompanied by double-pronged flower stalks that arise independently into the upper air each prong being 5 to 10cm (2 to 4in) long with white flowers notable for their scent and their purple-black anthers.

Nuphar advena is a more circumspect plant than our native yellow water lily *N. lutea* which would swamp most pools. The tiny *N.pumila* is much smaller. Below the water are bright thin leaves that look attractive, on the water surface it manages a few small shiny green floating ones and lots of tiny rounded golden flowers. Those of *N.advena* are much larger at 5 to 7cm (2 to 3in) across, and its leaves, cordate in shape, will rise energetically half out of the water.

A handsome-leaved plant that will produce a most unusual display of blossom is *Orontium aquaticum,* the golden club. In deep water the leaves float on the surface, the largest being 30cm (1ft) long and not quite half as wide, smaller ones may be only 12cm (5in) long. They are shaped rather like hosta leaves and are coloured a blue-green with a glaucous finish. In shallower water, or growing in the muddy waterside, the leaves point outwards and up and still look healthy and attractive. In late spring and through early summer a series of stems appear pointing outwards and from 15 to 60cm (6in to 2ft) long. They are brownish and flattened, especially above and, after growing clear of the leaves, they turn upwards, and become white below the golden yellow tip 2 to 5cm (1 to 2in) long. The white section of the stem is as long as the topmost part that looks as if it had been dipped into a pot of paint; this yellow is the result of lots of tiny yellow flowers. After the flowers have finished the leaves remain pleasant, the length emphasised by the many longitudinal veins.

A Shortlist of Moisture-loving Foliage Plants

Astilboides tabularis
Gunnera manicata
Hostas
Iris foetidissima 'Variegata'
Osmunda regalis

Rodgersia podophylla
Sagittaria sagittifolia plena
Scirpus tabernaemontanii 'Zebrinus'
Typha minima

10 *Covering the Ground*

Hobby gardening is beset with fashions. Some are dictated by changing economic and environmental factors. Self-sufficiency and rows of cabbages are the vogue one moment, but then heathers and conifers become the in-thing. A few persuasive writers can start a fashion or give a trend a helpful push. A decade or more ago the cry was, 'Plant ground covers.' The argument was beautifully simple: Nature abhors a vacuum, it does not leave soil bare. In our gardens we too should see to it that the soil was covered. After all, the more we cover the soil, the less space there will be for weeds. The aesthetic and the practical combined forcefully.

Articles and books proliferated on the virtues of ground-cover plants. The arguments were not without point, but the advocacy often went to extremes. Lists of plants lauded for their ground-covering potential included some that were certainly proficient in this but were most certainly not amongst the world's most exciting plants. Even more often the definition of a ground-covering plant was so elastic as to include many old friends that we had been growing as conventional plants for years and that we were surprised now to find described as 'ground coverers'.

The fact is that a garden is an unnatural creation; we work with Nature as much as is possible, but we are fighting Nature and her ground elder all the time. It is perfectly legitimate to maintain some part of the ground clear of plant life; the soil frames the plants and, like a frame around a picture, can enhance and concentrate our vision of it. Open soil can help drainage and create a warmer environment to benefit some plants. Having said that, there is no doubt that the ground-covering arguments brought forward several worthwhile plants and made us look at many others in a fresh light. As it is by their foliage that these plants carry out their territorial duties, in a book about foliage we must welcome the fashion.

A balance needs to be struck between beauty and utility. Covering the ground presents no problem, there are plenty of energetic plants to do that; we shall weigh the balance heavily in favour of beauty, concentrating first on plants that do well in the shade and create interest and cover in situations others would find difficult or impossible.

In the Shade
The woodland floor is the natural habitat of many ground coverers that happily accept shaded positions even if they are not under trees. They can be used with good effect between shrubs and by their contrasting foliage highlight the beauty of both. In a small garden it is difficult to make wide drifts of ground-covering plants, but it is worth trying to establish a reasonable stretch of one type before it meets another colonising plant.

Tiarella cordifolia has a mound of light-green cordate leaves enhanced by light airy sprays of creamy-white spring flowers. The leaves, somewhat like those of currants, become bronze coloured in autumn and winter. Sometimes the hairy leaves and stems become red, especially at the leaf margins. The dark-bronze colour seems to sink into the embossed network of veins leaving the upper portions still green. This soft-leaved plant may meet a drift of one with a highly polished reflective surface, a creeping variegated ivy, a taller rodgersia, or a variegated periwinkle.

Towards the front of any planting, one of the epimediums makes a pleasing drift of foliage quite distinct from the tiarella; where that it soft and hairy, the epimedium is polished and flat surfaced, the outline of the leaf is a clearly drawn arrowhead shape. Leaf blades are held horizontally on stems 20 to 50cm (8 to 20in) high, these stems as fine as threads giving the impression that the leaves are floating in the air. There are several rather similar species and forms but, as so often is the case, it is wisest to keep to one kind per drift. Leaves are topped by pretty little flowers in early spring. *Epimedium alpinum* produces its foliage towards the end of March, folded and held by pinky-red slender stalks at a height of 15 to 20cm (6 to 8in). They unfold to a pleasing light green but this is tinged bronze around the margins. As they age, the leaves become darker, and as there is usually a succession of leaves being produced there is an attractive tonal pattern. With the autumn and colder weather the leaves turn first to bronze, fawn, and yellow shades with the veins being etched

Epimedium x rubrum, one of a series of foliage plants that are much used in shady places but which will do well in more open areas. Evergreen leaves take on bronzy shades with age and winter

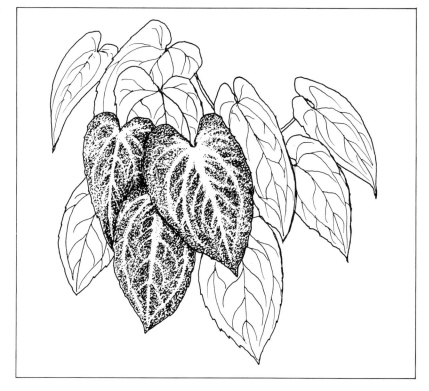

through the colours. The leaves maintain a reddish-bronze through-out winter.

Epimedium grandiflorum is a bolder plant but of a similar de-sign. This one stands 20 to 35cm (8 to 15in) high with stems carry-ing two or three widely spaced leaflets each 5 to 7cm (2 to 3in) long and heart shaped. The leaf surfaces are polished, particularly in the dwarfer form, *E.grandiflorum* 'Violaceum'. Through spring to summer a light shower of flowers is borne aloft, white or pale yellow with pink or violet petals.

The hybrid series *E.x versicolor* is from *E.grandiflorum x E.pin-natum colchicum,* and makes a show early in the year with open showers of pink and lemon flowers. The heart-shaped leaves follow a month or so later in April and are green and reddish bronze. The amount of the bronze colouring varies with different clones, some having a central green area by the leaf stalk with the green working its way up the sides of the veins.

Plants like the epimediums have creeping rootstocks well adapted to forming colonies, lily-of-the-valley will do likewise and form such a thick mass of foliage that a weed will have difficulty growing. *Caulophyllum thalictrioides* has a rhizomatous rootstock and starts into growth with dark-green endeavour that does not give much hint of the subtle light-green leaves that it will then unfold to mimic those of thalictrums. These are about 20 to 25cm (8 to 10in) high with little clouds of tiny pale purple-lilac flowers above. The plants grow larger, but it may be sensible to divide the rhizomes in early spring and plant the divisions some 25cm (10in) apart and so more quickly establish a drift.

Clumps of hostas can legitimately be classed as ground covering; established masses of *Hosta sieboldiana* 'Elegans' will not brook in-terference by any other vegetable life form. Such plants can make a needful contrast to one of the invasive but pleasing periwinkles like *Vinca major* 'Variegata' with polished leaves of dark green and cream. Few plants grow so easily in deep shade as these periwinkles, the variegated ones help to bring light into darkness.

There are places for bolder plants. The bergenias are tough customers ready to accept the worst of winter as well as displaying their rounded tough leaves throughout the rest of the year. At any time a few leaves will be completing their span on a clump, and these often become suffused with rich crimson, whilst the rest maintain a much lacquered rich green. The leaf colour depends on the cultivar or form; some are inclined to have coloured leaves year round, some will use the colour like a light touch of make-up while others paint themselves quite vividly. One of the strongest and largest is 'Ballawley', with the reverse of the leaves just as lacquered but a crimson reflection of the dark colouring of the 60cm (2ft) high, richly coloured branched flowerheads.

Possibly the most commonly seen bergenia is *B.cordifolia* with rounded green leaves just lightly touched with red. Its 35cm (15in) high fans of pink flowers give the clue — usually the darker the flowers the more likely the foliage is to be reddened. *B.c.* 'Purpurea'

has darker flowers and the leaves have a purplish red cast. All the bergenias are bold, strong plants, their rounded or heart-shaped leaves being up to 20cm (8in) across, and looking all the more robust if contrasted with the small-leaved tiarellas, with finely cut ferns, or even with small-leaved ivies.

Whilst it is not evergreen like bergenias, I enjoy the foliage of *Brunnera macrophylla* to such an extent that any seedlings found around an old clump are likely to be transferred elsewhere. Now we have it growing in the shade and in the open in all manner of sites. The winter sees the old leaves dead and blackened but in the centre of the clump there are usually a few small, rounded heart-shaped leaves only a centimetre or two across; they await the spring when the plants produce large wide mounds of beautiful, broad, heart-shaped light-green leaves, each growing now to perhaps 15cm (6in) across and making a plant pattern some 45cm (18in) high and twice as wide. The leaves have a mat finish and are attractively reticulate with the impressed network of veins. The many stems of widely branched tiny forget-me-not flowers in bright light blue are a pleasing bonus in early summer and then, if cut away, this may be paid yet again in the autumn, albeit in lesser quantities.

Creeping over the ground and smothering any impediment to their progress we can use one or more ivies. As they are mentioned in the chapter on climbers we can move on. There are of course other creeping plants capable of making excellent ground cover and providing interesting attractive foliage. In moist soils the

Brunnera macrophylla, a useful easy plant for shade or sun. It will do well on very poor soil

LEFT
Moisture-loving trio: blue-flowered *Iris chrysographes*, dwarf silver-grey *Salix lanata*, and monkey musk *Mimulus*

OPPOSITE
Delightful interplay of form, colour and texture. One of the newer cultivars *Hosta* 'Anticipation', with *Carex elata* 'Aurea', and the royal fern *Osmunda regalis*

sprawling stems of *Houttuynia cordata* 'Variegata' hold broadly ovate or somewhat heart-shaped leaves whose basic blue-green has given way, in two-thirds of its area, to cream and pinky-red segments. We have grown it both in sun and shade with equally good results, but it seems to be best in a somewhat sheltered environment and even then will not often get above some 15 to 20cm (6 to 8in) high.

If you have the right spot you might try a woodland plant from North America and quickly be convinced that you have a foliar star. This is *Diphylleia cymosa,* a herbaceous woodlander that is all drama. In late April, the thick creeping rhizomes throw up leaves all shining copper orange in their youth. It seems in a hurry, the flower buds can be seen close to the ground. Expansion is quick; within three weeks to a month the leaves have opened out to a theatrical 30 to 60cm (1 to 2ft) width, unusually divided into two halves by a deep central cut and with the two parts strongly serrated and marked by perhaps five or seven pointed lobes. The width of these leaves is such that the plant has been commonly called the umbrella leaf. Stems are run up 60cm to 1m (2 to 3ft) with a couple of similar but smaller leaves below the loose heads of simple white starry flowers. The fruits that follow are light blue. It needs to be grown in good soil that is moist in a spot that has plenty of shelter and some dappled shade. The height of the plants will reflect the situation in which they find themselves, in a drier spot the plants will make only half of their potential 1m height.

It is no great jump from the last to the podophyllums, they are closely related. These are foliage plants for the moist shaded areas. It is a small family of which there are three species at least in cultivation. The American mandrake is *P.peltatum.* The daffodils are just getting into full swing when this plant begins to rouse itself, a couple of white shoots appear above ground and then two hanging leaves on compressed stalks looking almost fungoid, like mushrooms. Leaves with a conspicuous white patch at the leaf stalk are unfurled as rounded seven- or nine-lobed wonders often over 30cm (1ft) wide. Each flower stem produces two bronzed leaves folded together and in these junctions are hidden white flowers that are followed by oval fruits in July — which seems a sensible enough time but makes the common name, May apple, a little difficult to understand. The fruit is red but also hidden. *P.hexandrum* (formerly *P.emodii*) has massive glossy leaves boldly serrated. They may be 25 to 50cm (10 to 20in) across. Stems may carry them in sheltered spots to a height of 1 to 2m (3 to 6ft). As the young deflexed leaves are pulled upright and opened, the bright green may be marked with paler blotches. The leaves of *P.versipelle* are scarcely any smaller and will take on a reddish cast as they mature.

In the Sun — the Heather Garden

Many of the plants already mentioned in the previous section are as happy in sun as in shade. Some plants hate shade. Heathers live in the open, demanding sun and light. Without it, the leaf colour of many heathers will not develop properly.

The widest spectrum is available by using both the lime tolerant and the lime-hating types, but even for soils with free lime the range of heathers is surprisingly wide. They all seem to look the better for being associated with dwarf conifers, and this helps to widen the design possibilities.

The use of heathers in the garden may be viewed in several ways. They are ideal for ground covering as they make such dense growth that, if the ground is clear of weed to start with, there is little danger of fresh incursions. They are undemanding plants that flourish in almost any soil and indeed are often at their best in poor soils. Their mode of growth with small healthy foliage makes them ideal plants to contrast with broad-leaved plants. They will integrate with the multi-generic society of mixed beds and borders and are best placed to the sunny forefront to give evergreen cover throughout the year.

The planting of three plants of a kind produces a total effect in the garden greater than three times the effect of just one and this applies especially when planting heathers.

The main lime-tolerant species is *E. herbacea (E. carnea)* and to this varied kind may be added the hybrid *E. x darleyensis* and its kin. Other lime-tolerant kinds include some of the best hybrids listed as *E. hybrida,* together with the *E. erigena* and *E. arborea* clans. Whilst they are lime tolerant, they like the addition of peat around their roots. Lime-tolerant kinds flower in winter and this makes them particularly welcome.

The summer-flowering *E. cinerea, E. tetralix, E. vagans,* and *Calluna vulgaris,* all hate lime. The planting of one of these, bought for very little, may indicate the presence or absence of lime more cheaply than a soil-testing kit!

The arrangement of heathers to create a pleasing picture of foliage is not difficult. The main element of the picture is going to be colour, both of foliage and flower. The leaves may be thought rather uniform, but this is not really the case as there is a wide difference between the narrow needles of such as *E. herbacea* and the tufted foliage of the wild ling, *Calluna vulgaris.* Differences of texture, of brilliance, and of plant mass can be exploited. The height of some *E. arborea* forms reaching 1.6 to 2m (5 to 6ft) can give a fine sense of scale, as can the dwarf conifers that blend happily into the plan.

The idea of a heather garden as another form of bedding out must be resisted; we are trying to create a miniature landscape not a flat, multicoloured carpet. We want to vary the colours, heights, shapes, and atmosphere. The lie of the ground may lend greater drama. A slight rise may be emphasised by siting taller growing kinds there above some that hug the ground. Planting in groups of a kind will fairly quickly give a finished natural cover as the plants grow into each other; you may be tempted to buy equal numbers of each chosen variety. This could work out perfectly all right, but in any larger scheme the same-sized groupings of different types may look suspiciously contrived. Better to have three of a kind here, with seven of another, and nine of a third, and five of a fourth. Of course any such apparently random planting will be well thought out to contrast foliage colour, flower colour, blooming time and height, with consideration given to the spreading potential of each type.

Visit some established heather plantings before starting your own. You may see effective groupings and spot others you might wish to avoid. Whilst the heather garden may be ninety per cent heathers and conifers, a useful foliar and floral contrast can be achieved by adding dwarf bulbs and rhizomatous plants (for instance Erythroniums and Trilliums) as well as some broader-leaved small shrubs — perhaps one or two of the attractively leaved rhododendrons. Then visit one of the nurseries specialising in heathers and pick out the kinds that you want, together with some free advice.

Erica herbacea (E. carnea) has several yellow-leaved forms, 'Foxhollow' is a golden-green, vigorous one with relatively large leaves, 'Ann Sparkes' is another with darker carmine flowers. *E. h.* 'Aurea' has rich yellow leaves, lightly green tinted and grows to 15 to 20cm (6 to 8in) high but many times wider. These would contrast with some of the darker ones like the low-growing *E. h.* 'Vivellii' with black-green leaves and dark-red flowers. This is a healthy kind but spreads rather more slowly so you may plant five to give the effect of three of another type. Others like 'King George' grow rampantly reaching 20 to 25cm (8 to 10in) upwards and spreading easily to 1m (3ft) with healthy foliage. 'Springwood White', whilst spreading rapidly, keeps low to make pale yellowy-green cover.

The series gathered under the *E. hybrida* flag are taller, dark-leaved kinds. 'Arthur Johnston' makes a 45cm (18in) high rounded mound of close dark leaves with long flower spikes in rose pink. Whilst the *E. herbacea* kinds bloom from December till March, hybridas tend to open a little later and span the months February to May. 'Silver Beads' (Siberschmelze) has very dark foliage to contrast with snow-white blossom. Pink-flowered 'Jenny Porter' is paler in leaf, with the new growing tips cream. 'J. W. Porter' has the young foliage painted red.

The famous hybrid *Erica x darleyensis* is the name now used to cover several plants of similar parentage. They are strong-growing, wide-spreading heathers, perhaps 35cm (15in) high and several times wider. The dark 'Darley Dale' is accompanied from November till May by an abundant succession of lilac-pink blossom, half a year in flower cannot be bad. The cultivar 'Margaret Porter' spreads well, but only reaches some 20cm (8in) in height. 'Ghost Hills' has good rich foliage but has some seasonal variation, the young spring growth is creamy.

Flowering succession is carried a little further forward by the *E. erigena* cultivars; starting in March they last into May. 'W. T. Rackliffe' grows to 65cm (2ft) with rich, green, compact foliage and white flowers. 'Golden Lady' is a most lovely contrast with bright, almost luminous lemon leaves. It grows steadily, looking vivid and lively at all times, its floral impact is insignificant, a meagre few white bits. A contrast is the popular rather erect bushy 'Brightness', a name that refers more to the red flowers than the foliage of a dark bronze-green.

Taller by far are *E.arborea, E.australis,* and *E.lusitanica.* They build up considerable cloud-shaped forms some 1.6 to 2m (5 to 6ft) high. *E.arborea* 'Alpina' makes a good tall shrub of healthy green and has fragrant white blossom from March till May. There are golden-leaved kinds in 'Albert's Gold' and 'Estrella Gold', while 'Gold Tips' is rich green with the young growing ends golden. All are white flowered. *E.lusitanica* varies the pattern slightly by having pink buds that open white. *E.australis* is similar in form with rosy flowers from April till June.

Lime-hating Heathers

The foliage of both *E.cinerea* and *E.tetralix* tends to be smaller even than that of those already mentioned. The Scottish bell heather, *E.cinerea,* encompasses a huge gamut of leaf colours. 'Eden Valley' is pale flowered and pale-green leaved, only 15cm (6in) high and in bloom from June through to September. 'Golden Hue' has bright golden-green foliage, whilst 'Golden Drop' is old gold to copper coloured. 'Pink Ice' is very dark, rather like 'Velvet Night' whose dark leaves are combined with purple flowers, the darkest of any heather.

E. tetralix, the cross-leaved heath, has its little leaves arranged in outward-pointing whorls of four, to give a square set, more stylish look. The leaves are glaucous, some being very noticeably so. 'Pink Star' is low growing with grey leaves, 'Alba Mollis' is silvery and larger both in stature, at 22cm (9in), and in its white flowers. These are spreading shrubs with relatively large nodding round flowers in bunches held above the plant.

The most exciting foliage is to be found amongst the hugely variable *Calluna vulgaris,* the ling. Sizes, shapes, colours are endlessly permutated. 'Foxii Nana' makes miniature hummocks only a tight 10cm (4in) high. They could have been designed as pin cushions in bright green. 'Humpty Dumpty' is even more vividly green and only one size larger at 15cm (6in). Others make low wide plants, 'Golden Carpet', true to its name, is completely earthbound and establishes a golden carpet pile only 5 to 7cm (2 to 3in) thick, the gold suffused with orange and red. 'Ruth Sparkes' is one of a number of golden forms, this one growing to about 22cm (9in). Some are silver grey like 'Anthony Davis', but probably the most popular are those that, at midsummer, can be an almost uniform gold, but, in winter, ignite into fiery oranges and reds. 'Robert Chapman' is one that stands an impressive 45cm (18in); 'Spitfire' at 30cm (12in) is another; dressed gold in summer, it dons a rich red coat for winter. The choice seems almost endless. 'Golden Feather' is a good descriptive name for a 45cm (18in) one devoid of flowers. For ages the leading flowering calluna has been 'H.E.Beale' with long, up-ward-pointing spikes of double round rosy flowers like so many little beads. Whilst the flowers are wonderful, the dark grey-green foliage is less exciting.

There are many outstanding callunas, but one called *C.v.multi-color* takes a lot of bettering. It forms neat masses 22cm (9in) high, vividly coloured in yellows, oranges and reds. Bright at all times, in the winter it starts to glow with an astonishing influorescence in psychedelic pinky oranges and reds. It really does look as though the tiny leaves generate their own light. The leaves are minuscule, only to .1 to 1.3cm ($\frac{1}{20}$ to $\frac{1}{8}$in) long but crowded along the many stems so that the plant looks well dressed and in good order.

Conifers combine naturally with heathers, the junipers associate with heathers in the wild. These have been listed in previous chapters. The prostrate forms are wonderfully efficient at ground covering, keeping weed firmly at bay. The blue-green and silver of some clones make an interesting change of colour in the heather garden. Upright junipers and other conifers may be used to break up the horizontal monopoly. The conical *Thuja occidentalis* 'Rheingold' is one of the best known and is pleasing in its even shape and golden colouring of spring and summer. It adopts a richer orange-old gold for the winter. Like many of the 'dwarfs' it can eventually make a sizeable tree head high or more, but it is so slow growing it is unlikely to cause any problems of scale for many years after planting. It looks good and well mannered from small specimen until venerable old age.

Rampaging evergreen periwinkle *Vinca major* 'Variegata' builds up a thick cover over the ground

11   *Up the Walls and Clematis All*

OVERLEAF
The deciduous maxi-leaved
vine *Vitis coignetiae* in
company with dark
evergreen *Clematis armandii*
which has creamy flowers
turning pink, in spring
(Overbecks)

We make too little use of our walls in the garden. Why this should be is difficult to establish clearly. There is a prejudice against ivy and other self-adhesive plants on the grounds that they damage the mortar or keep the walls wet. Neither of these charges is likely to be proved. Modern mortar will not be spoilt by ivy or any other climbing plant and cover of ivy will certainly keep the wall drier and warmer.

With the shrinking size of modern gardens it may be argued that house walls offer much needed extra room to grow plants. The interest in hanging baskets suggests that the extra space would be welcomed. Whilst there are houses where it may be wrong to crowd the walls with plants, most would be vastly improved and made more interesting. The vertical is a whole new dimension waiting to be exploited.

Choose how much wall to cover, and then select the plants, perhaps even some that would be impossible in the open. The base of a wall that receives sunshine can be used to encourage slightly tender herbaceous and bulbous plants as well as climbing shrubs.

Some plants appreciate the support afforded by walls while others may enjoy their proximity merely because they give them shelter and extra warmth. The evergreen *Magnolia grandiflora* will be one of these and a fine foliage plant. Its simple large leaves are a rich green, well polished and making a dense cover. The underside of the leaves is a rusty-orange brown felt. In cooler parts of the country some of the camellias, both the *C. reticulata* and *C. japonica* kinds, will benefit from the shelter and warmth of a wall. Their dark, healthy, tough evergreen foliage will lend a high-class respectability.

In all, except the mildest parts of the country, *Fremontodendron californicum* is going to need the aid and comfort of a wall. It is grown for its very bright, polished, wide open golden flowers in May and June, but its foliage is interesting. Leaves are 5 to 10cm (2 to 4in) long and can be as wide, or nearly so. They are rounded in form but showing three lobes in the smaller ones, and perhaps up to seven in the bigger ones. The soft mid-green has a matt finish, hairy in youth, always rough to the touch, and with lower surfaces covered with a fawny white felt. The shrub-cum-tree is deciduous but may hang on to a proportion of the younger leaves through milder winters. Branches can be pinned to the wall and be pruned to make a neat arrangement. Root disturbance is resented.

The climbing *Hydrangea petiolaris* clamps itself to the masonry and soon leans over the guttering. Its deciduous green hydrangea leaves are pleasing enough; the creamy lace-cap flowers are produced in sufficient quantity to create a pretty picture, pretty with-

out being spectacular. *Schizophragma hydrangeoides* looks very similar with leaves 10 to 15cm (4 to 6in) long by 6 to 10cm (2½ to 4in) wide, rich green and boldly serrated. Flowers in flat bunches 20 to 25cm (8 to 10in) across are creamy yellow.

The beautifully leaved *Actinidia chinensis* has already been lauded in the first chapter. It is well worth wall space for its unusual foliage. Other candidates clamouring for space include many that are very attractive in flower, fruit, and autumn colouring, but with foliage that is adequate rather than inspiring. Such plants would include the winter jasmine, *J.nudiflorum, Forsythia suspensa,* the pyracanthas, the ceanothus hybrids, many roses, and most of the honeysuckles.

Clematis

The clematies are a large genus; many species have very appealing foliage, the large-flowered hybrids on the whole being the least well favoured in this respect. In full growth many look very attractive with neatly divided pointed leaves. The deciduous ones can look rather gaunt as naked tangles in the winter, and some are distinctly shabby in the first part of winter when much of the foliage is dead and blackened but is held onto instead of being shed.

Clematis armandii's behaviour is above reproach. It maintains a dark evergreen cloak of leaves kept in impeccable, polished good order. Individually leaflets measure 7 to 15cm (3 to 6in) by 2 to 6cm (1 to 2½in). They are clean cut and marked by three veins. Flowers appear in spring, usually three to a cluster, each being 5 to 6cm (2 to 2½in) across. They start life either an unsullied white or a cream, but they blush to a rosy pink as they mature.

C.cirrhosa balearica is another evergreen species that will need the warmth of a wall to do well. It is listed in some catalogues as the fern leaved clematis, and the much divided, narrowly fragmented leaves have a fern-like appeal. The major leaves are deeply cut into lobes and these are again divided into slender points, the minor leaves being cut into three or five strong pointed lobes. The rich green of summer becomes a purple bronze in winter, a most pleasing winter foliage. During spells of milder weather the bronze is likely to be accompanied by a welcome scatter of four petalled creamy flowers some 5cm (2in) across. *C.cirrhosa* the close evergreen relative is not so interesting or good looking

The masses of *C.montana* that scramble decoratively over walls, sheds, garages, and clamber through trees, are glorious in their abundant blossoming, but their energetic twisting climbing habit and their foliage also draw admiration. Leaves are on a sensible smallish scale, three pointed leaflets to each, and each leaflet with a few sharp serrations. The colour is usually a green, more or less suffused with pink purple. When it has finished with its leaves in the autumn, it sheds them quickly and completely. *C.tangutica* is similarly well behaved, but its convoluted tangle of branches is decorated with many bunches of seedheads, silky feathery tassels that glint in the light. It can rival old man's beard in the hedgerow. This is

the best of the yellow species, parading a whole succession of bright flowers all through autumn until winter is imminent. Petals join to make an urn shape with their pointed tips recurving outwards. The foliage is prolific, a bright green with just a light greyish cast over it. Each leaf is usually divided into three separated leaflets which are sometimes lobed and always strongly cut with pointed serrations. The effect is of a cheerful, energetic, healthy, self-contained character.

Vines

The vines and their relatives can be marvellous on walls. Nothing is too high for them. Their one weakness, if it should be deemed such, is that they are deciduous. The huge-leaved *Vitis coignetiae* has already been mentioned. With undivided leaves capable at times of reaching 30cm (1ft) long by 25cm (10in) wide it is unlikely to be overlooked. Of the true vines, *V.vinifera* 'Purpurea' is outstanding as a foliage plant. Its leaves start out a wonderful red wine colour, which matures to a rich maroon and then to a dark purple, sometimes with a little white fluff on its surface. Leaves are well displayed: they are flat and the most is made of their decorative Corinthian outline. The typical vineleaf shape has been redrawn more surely with three or five lobes and with these boldly cut into a scalloped serration, altogether most decorative. Few can rival the richness and depth of the colouring, and this, combined with the attractive leaf form, makes it dramatic against a wall or wherever it is allowed to twist its way. Tight bunches of small dark fruit are covered with a blue white bloom and decorate its branches for many weeks in late autumn.

Parthenocissus tricuspidata with its self-adhesive tipped tendrils is the most popular of climbing vines. often called Virginia creeper, although this name is really the property of *P.quinquefolia*, another brilliant autumn colourer

The plant with the right to the name Virginia creeper is *Parthenocissus quinquefolia,* but a group of related plants seem to have acquired the name by common use. Perhaps we should be more specific in our use of common names. Both *P.quinquefolia* and *P.tricuspidata* have tendrils with tips with adhesive discs. Once a young plant has a few of these discs in place, growth will be rapid. *P.t.* 'Veitchii' has already been noted for its foliage. The glossy leaves are a picture through the summer, in autumn they are, I think, easily the most richly coloured of all the plants. Leaves are dropped within a few days.

It would be a shame not to have the Virginia creeper or a relative growing up the walls, but it would be wise to plant them where the foliage could be enjoyed and where winter nudity will not be noticeable.

Ivies

Ivy may sound dull, but many kinds have really beautiful foliage that is all too often overlooked. Ivies have the benefit of being evergreen and generally having constitutions of unbeatable hardiness. Although evergreen, those with patterned surfaces often change colour quite considerably with the coming of autumn frosts.

Of course, some ivies are so large and so brightly coloured we

cannot ignore them. *Hedera colchica* 'Dentata Variegata' and *H. canariensis* 'Gloire de Marengo', are popular variegated kinds that are marvellous value where a bold effect is required. The common ivy *Hedera helix* might seem unexciting to the casual onlooker, but one's attitude might change when told that there are at present at least 330 varieties of this species on sale. Some nurserymen specialise in ivies; one in Essex does nothing else. One of the most popular cultivars at present is 'Goldheart', also known as 'Jubilee', with well-lobed, highly polished small leaves with centres a shining rich yellow. The leaf surfaces of others can be patterned by areas of green, cream or white, and pinky red. Others, such as 'Luzii', confine their patterning to shades of green and white, but the number of subtle attractive changes of tone to be achieved by such cultivars well repays close inspection. Visit a good collection and choose the colour and leaf size you want. Nothing grows easier; you should choose exactly what you want as it could be with you for decades.

Hedera helix 'Goldstern', *H.h.* 'Sagittifolia Variegata', *H.h.* 'Goldheart', *H.h.* 'Buttercup', *H. canariensis* 'Gloire de Marengo', *H. colchica* 'Dentata Variegata'

A marriage of stone with *Hedera helix* 'Minor Marmorata Aurea' and the contained *Sedum bithynicum aurea (Herterton House)*

12 *The Minuscule*

Size by itself does not guarantee value, neither is small necessarily especially beautiful. We are amazed by the gunnera's huge architecture and are intrigued by the efficiency of a raoulia with leaves as big as a pin head. Few of us can afford space for super large things, we can all grow many of the miniature plants even without a proper garden. The alpines and other tiny plants that can be grown in troughs or other containers may have foliage as lovely as any of the larger plants. Here is a chance to have a wide variety of foliage within a limited area. When examining these small plants we realise that there is greater diversity here than in any other gardening realm.

Most of the larger plants have tiny forms. Conifers and trees do a natural bonzai act. There are miniature irises, tulips, daffodils, and lots of other bulbous forms, some surprisingly attractive in their foliage. There are hardy plants with succulent leaves like the large sempervivum and sedum genera grown primarily for their foliage. There are cushion- and mat-forming silver-leaved plants, many from New Zealand, from whence come also an extraordinary range of little shrubs, hebes and others, that we are only just beginning to appreciate. Some primulas have their leaves ornamented with gold and silver dust; a whole section of the saxifrage genus has leaves intriguingly encrusted so that they often glitter with silver. There are the hairy and the clean-shaven, the orthodox green and the unusually coloured, the plain and the variegated, the deciduous and the evergreen, the bold and the fragile, the easy and the challenging. All the plant world is here.

Age, like income tax, is a problem that will not go away. As we become older the physical effort needed to keep the garden in order may become subject to the inexorable laws of diminishing returns. We adapt by growing more small plants in containers, sinks, trough, or raised beds designed to bring the working level up.

Sempervivums and Sedums

Collections of sempervivums and sedums can offer endless opportunity for creating mosaics of differing shapes, sizes, colours and textures. The sempervivums with their immaculately arranged rosettes are foliage plants whose floral effects may appeal, but are short-lived. The rosettes may measure as much as those of 'Commander Hay' some 20cm (8in) across or just the few millimetres of some of the tiny *S. arachnoideum* forms. They can be a uniform rich green or coloured wholly or partially with orange, red or purple. They may be hairy or polished, or intriguingly decorated with gossamer like the *S. arachnoideums.* Some of the most effective are clearly bicolored with grey-green leaves whose pointed tips are painted purplish red, or others that are basically red but are green at their bases.

A trio of rock-garden plants, the fleshy *Sempervivum tectorum* (back), dark-leaved *Ajuga reptans* 'Purpurea', and *Sedum spathulifolium* 'Purpureum' (front)

Some of the smaller sedums produce a cluster of rosettes similar in general effect to those of the sempervivums. The popular and easy *Sedum spathulifolium* will quickly establish a series of flat rosettes of fleshy leaves but, whilst the sempervivums' leaves are wide at the base and usually come to a definite point, those of these sedums are spatulate, their greatest width being at their ends. *S. spathulifolium* is a variable plant, the size of the leaves may vary, but its most changeable aspect is the colour. There are uniform purplish-red forms, green ones, grey ones, and some thickly covered with sparkling white bloom. Normal rosettes are about 2.5cm (1in) across but the green *S. s.* 'Majus' can be much wider, perhaps double the width like the purple red *S. s.* 'Purpureum' with its mealy white young leaves.

The stonecrop, *Sedum acre,* is a weed. Every fleshy little leaf is a potential new plant. We allow space to a few varieties, *S. s.* 'Elegans' is slightly variable but the usual form is a rampant little plant with lots of fat small succulent leaves and stems all in a shining blue-white. Winter may bring a touch of rosy purple. One variation is a most lovely soft emerald green. Bits of this plant may break off or be scattered by birds, and start new mats wherever they fall. Other sedums are more circumspect, they have central rootstocks from which a series of stems arise and fan out to make an even low rounded mass of attractive foliage. *S. aizoon* is one such, usually with fleshy serrated leaves flushed with wine red. *S. middendorfianum* is similar but a slimline version.

Bugles

Not all dwarf plants are alpines. The bugle, *Ajuga reptans*, of our meadows has produced some finely coloured forms, especially useful as they are evergreen and completely untouched by winter weather. *A. reptans* makes a shining mat pressed close to the ground. The type is green, sometimes suffused with bronze. The garden kinds are of various colours with one or two brightly varieg-ated clones. The most common, marketed as *A.r.*'Variegata' or *A.r.*'Argentea', is brightly painted with splashes of white and cream. Plants sold as *A.r.*'Tricolor' and *A.r.*'Multicolor' and some labelled 'Rainbow' may be the same or similar clones. In winter the leaves tend to be a dark beetroot colour with paler edges; in the growing season they are a jigsaw of green, pink, red, and sometimes white patches. Particularly effective, especially in winter, is *A.r.*'Atropur-purea' which can make a carpet of polished leaves of very dark purple-bronzes, maybe 1m (3ft) wide and rarely more than 2.5cm (1in) high. Leaves are rounded and crinkled enough for light to play on them, each 2.5 to 5cm (1 to 2in) across. The much bracted 12cm (5in) spikes of mint-like purple flowers add to the attraction of this easy plant. The more light it has, the deeper the leaf colour; in shade it tends to become green.

The thymes are pleasant little things; the most worthwhile for leaves are the silver and golden variegated forms, *Thymus x cit-riodorus* 'Silver Queen' and *T.x.c.* 'Golden King.' This last is a most useful plant. Little rooted pieces can be poked into odd spots safe in the knowledge that they will flourish and create neat, little-leaved mats of foliage, two-thirds gold, one-third green.

Silver and Pewter

Some of the really dwarf dianthus species and first generation hybrids make very neat rounded low mats of narrow grey-green pointed leaves. They are good in the winter, though more silvery grey in summer.

The wide low mounds of mossy saxifrages are neat, bright, and lively in winter and throughout the year. The many rosettes of little leaves, usually of three narrow pointed lobes, build up into a pleas-ant picture, quite distinct and more vividly verdant than other saxif-rage types. *S.x.* 'Tumbling Waters' and its kin have metallic-coloured strong leaves, long narrow oblong ones arranged in low-centred rosettes. Each leaf can be 2.5 to 5cm (1 to 2in) long, their basic grey-green enlivened with the many silver-white encrusted spots that

BELOW LEFT
Two smaller plants, the neat *Saxifraga umbrosa* and the marble-leaved *Cyclamen hederifolium* (*C.neapolitanum*)

BELOW RIGHT
Creeping grey-leaved *Acaena novae-zelandiae* with miniature rose leaves, grey-green *Antennaria parviflora* (centre) and bright-green mossy saxifrage 'Pixie'

tightly line the margins. The flower sprays of myriad white stars are delivered on extraordinarily long arching stems like fountains some 30cm (1ft) high. Other hard-leaved saxifrages make neat mounds of tight silvery rosettes of similarly encrusted leaves but often only about 1cm (½in) long.

More silvery effects can be arranged by using easy hardy plants like *Antennaria parvifolia*. This is the smallest of the genus in cultivation. In winter the ground-hugging rosettes are grey-green, perhaps 4cm (1½in) across, with only the resting leaf bud being shiny silver white. In the growing part of the year the fresh narrow leaves, oblong or somewhat spatulate, are silvered. Little heads of pink flowers, like refined groundsels, tend to enhance the silver effect. Whilst this keeps hard to the ground, the relative *A.dioica* is rather larger and more variable. Its height may be 5 to 30cm (2 to 12in). This species forms larger mats of woolly spatulate leaves 4cm (1½in) long. Whiteish or pale pink groundsel-like flowers are very much pinker in the form *rosea*. The amount of woolliness of the leaves varies, some being as thickly covered above as below, but most are distinctly more thickly covered underneath. Some forms come close to the squat and small sized 'Aprica'.

While plants like *A.parvifolia* press themselves to the ground, the raoulias seem to be at one with it. Though there are several small shrubby species of the family they tend to be difficult to grow, but the mat-forming kinds can be easy if provided with really good drainage. The genus is native to New Zealand and Australia. Stems

Sempervivums in frost

creep over the soil surface and the many tiny round leaves make a complete soil cover. *R. australis (R. hookeri)* manufactures a silver carpet of leaves scarcely more than .1cm ($^1/_{16}$ in) long to some that at .3cm ($^1/_8$ in) will be large. The silver colouring comes from silky hairs both on the upper and lower surfaces. In *R. glabra* the leaves are fractionally larger and the surface free, or nearly free, of hairs. In *R. subsericea* the effect is of a green carpet of leaves .2 to .6cm ($^1/_6$ to $^1/_4$ in) across; if an odd one curls, the under-surface will be seen to be white with hairs.

Most primulas have good workaday leaves. They look healthy and do their duty, but they are rarely a feature in themselves. Some species are a little more special; *P. marginata* has firm small-scale, auricula-type leaves sometimes lightly dusted with farina over their surfaces and usually clearly marked with this meal along the leaf margins. The hybrid 'Linda Pope' can look a plant apart, its leaves somewhat serrated and heavily edged with pale golden meal. It is a splendid effect, especially in a large thriving clump. The heads of deep lavender-blue flowers are a pleasing complement to the leaves in the spring.

Many genera noted for their endeavour in other fields also contribute to things lowly. There are many small willow species and hybrids that either creep over the soil or grow only a few inches high. *Salix reticulata* is a joy. Firm dark stems are pressed to the ground. In winter the round leaf buds can be seen waiting to burst into growth. With spring the soft, silky leafy infancy is revealed. The leaves are unfurled, not like the standard willow, but tough ones, round as a table-tennis bat, may be wider than long. These leaves are a rich green, enlivened by a high gloss finish and an embossed network of veins to justify its name. Given a moist spot it will apply itself to spreading over ground and rock.

Salix lanata, the silver-leaved dwarf willow, has been mentioned before. One of the joys of an alpine enthusiast's collection could be a well-grown specimen of *Salix x boydii*. This natural hybrid was found in Scotland in 1901, the result of the somewhat disparate parents, the bushy *S. lanata* and the prostrate *S. reticulata*. All the *S. x boydii* in cultivation have arisen from that one hybrid which is a plant of great character, a very slow-growing, rigidly upright shrub or miniature tree with dark silver-grey leaves of very firm substance and almost perfectly circular. The leaves are so firm and strong that they could be artificial.

Most of these small plants will do well in trough or sink gardens. The old stone troughs that were once used on farms and elsewhere are now rare collectors' items. Good imitations can be made that soon look old. In these can be grown mixed collections of complementary plants. The soil mix in such restricted containers can be made to suit its occupants exactly and pH levels can be precise. Miniature arrangements of plants are always attractive but they can be especially welcome in poorer weather when the garden proper may be wet and inhospitable. They add great interest to the foreground of any garden.

13 Foliage for Cutting, and for Preserving

Winter foliage will be mainly from shrubs and trees. Lively colourful displays can be made using pieces of golden variegated *Elaeagnus pungens* 'Aureo Variegata', the metallic greys and silvers of eucalypts, the many colours and shades of pittosporums, and shoots of golden privet. Lemony scent from *Mahonia japonica* sprays is a pleasant bonus. The hybrids are also scented. Dark garrya leaves will be accompanied by their long grey-green tassels of catkins.

When spring is about to arrive there are leaves that look especially fine as they burst their winter buds; 'sticky buds', twigs of the horse chestnut, unfurl hairy stems and soft pale-green leaves. Stems and young leaves make a lovely picture. Whitebeam twigs have glistening silvery leaves. Whilst the slow-growing acers have gorgeous emerging foliage, you may not wish to sacrifice bits from your specimens. However, stronger acers are a different matter, twigs of these can be bewitching as coloured scales open and infant leaves make their way into the world.

Through spring, summer, and autumn there are always shrubs and trees from which to cut foliage. Bits of junipers and other conifers can be used without affecting the plants at all. Eucalypts grow so readily there is a continual supply of foliage. Coppiced *E.gunnii* will give a fountain of juvenile foliage with rounded leaves.

Herbaceous plants are useful with whatever flowers are in season. The hostas are obvious candidates. *Macleaya cordata* or *M.microcarpa* have wonderfully shaped and coloured foliage that will add distinction to any arrangement. Sword-like leaves of water-loving irises make useful strong material. Many ferns are most lovely.

Golden privet, *Ligustrum ovalifolium aureum*, with some leaves all pure gold and others green-margined gold, and the golden-edged box, *Buxus sempervirens* 'Marginata', so much more lively than the standard all-green type.

Preserving Foliage

Saving foliage is not that difficult, so that whatever the time of year or the weather outside, there is always a range of leaves or sprays of foliage waiting. Some dry almost naturally. Eucalypts, conifers, hebes, and hosta leaves placed in a vase with a little water may gradually dry in a warmish spot without shrivelling up. These may be brittle and need handling with care. The most popular preservative method uses glycerine.

An advantage with glycerine is that the leaves and stems retain a degree of suppleness. A possible disadvantage is that the leaves tend to change colour as they absorb the glycerine. Preserved beech leaves are very popular, they look well and are ideal for many floral and foliar arrangements. Many others are just as successful.

Additionally, in early spring when the sap is rising, it is worth trying bare-leaved twigs of the twisty willow, *Salix tortuosa*, the corkscrew hazel, and such things as pussy willow with their catkins, as these can be preserved intact for years. Very young leaves cannot be preserved this way, nor will success be achieved if leaves have become too old to take up moisture.

One part of glycerine is stirred vigorously in two parts of boiling water. The mixture is used warm. Stems are placed with their clean-cut bottoms in about 5cm (2in) of the solution and allowed to take this up for as long as is needed to get the leaves fully loaded. This will be indicated by the change of colour and is especially easy to see in the veins below most leaves. Keep an eye on the level of the solution so that more can be added if needed. Some of the tougher, thicker leaves will be the better for being wiped over with a cloth soaked in the solution both before and during the process. The length of time needed to glycerine leaves will vary according to the type and state of the leaves. It may be only a couple of days or as long as two weeks. If the stems are left in overlong you may see little globules of glycerine on the leaf surfaces. The stems should be removed immediately and the surfaces wiped clear of the glycerine, otherwise fungus may start to grow.

Once you are happy that the stems and leaves have been properly glycerined, take them from the solution and place them somewhere to dry off naturally. If there were some very young portions on the twigs that failed to be properly preserved, these can be cut away. Green colouring can be enhanced by incorporating some antifreeze in the solution or, failing this, some green ink. Rich coppery colours result from a crystal or two of permanganate of potash dissolved into the solution.

Some foliage can be glycerined by total immersion. Important items such as some ferns, hosta leaves, lily of the valley, violets, and tougher ones like bergenia and ivy can be done more successfuly this way. Having immersed the pieces completely, you will need to keep them down with plastic grid or something similar that will hold them under without distorting or breaking them. Eucalyptus can also be done this way. The leaves will be seen to be processed when the colour or tone has changed evenly. Remove them carefully, dry off the surplus solution with paper kitchen towelling, and leave to dry naturally.

Having successfully preserved the leaves or twigs, they should be stored somewhere dry. In a moist atmosphere the glycerine-loaded leaves will delight fungus spores.

One way of preserving autumn leaves is relatively simple. Clean, unmarked leaves are picked, and the leaves are carefully ironed both sides. A hot iron will drive the moisture from the leaves quite quickly and leave them crisp. They should then be carefully picked up and pressed under a pile of books for a few days. The result can be very attractive but the leaves are fragile. However, they can be arranged to great effect by being glued to a dry twig. The flat leaves give a stylised feel but as each leaf is in a different plane the total effect can be very intriguing.

Index